Contents

Coming In?

Let's not start with an argument. This is a guide to the Yorkshire coast so we had better clear up what we understand to be Yorkshire and what we understand the word coast to mean.

The easier one first then. Coast is generally defined as being that part of the land that is adjacent to (or very close to) the sea. A coastline is similarly accepted as being the place where land ceases and sea or ocean (or in some cases lake) starts. I do like how some dictionaries talk about the coastline in terms of the contour of a coast. This helps to picture the edges of land in terms of slope, and as with all contours – these vary considerably. In some places, such as Flamborough Head, sheer chalk cliffs give the coastline the steepest of contours, whilst at other places such as Spurn Point, the sea meets the land at such a shallow angle, it only takes one strong tidal surge for the North Sea to wash over the coastline and flood much of the peninsula.

Many dictionaries talk about coast purely in terms of seas and oceans, although Webster's dictionary does also include the possibility that lakes can be bordered by coastlines. Perhaps it is worth clearing up the difference between a sea and an ocean too. Especially since what is now accepted as the North Sea once commonly went by the name of the German Ocean. Most dictionaries make a simple distinction between seas and oceans – it is a question of size, apparently. The world's five largest expanses of water are all oceans, ranging in size from the Pacific (64 million square miles) to the Arctic Ocean (5 million square miles). The stretch of salt water that meets the Yorkshire coastline is the North Sea and is tiny in comparison, at a little under a quarter of a million square miles. The North Sea is also relatively shallow, with an average depth of 312 feet. Boulby Cliff, on the Cleveland Way near Staithes stands more than twice that height. The North Sea still has enough water in it to fill over 21.5 billion Olympic-sized swimming pools.

By the way, the North Sea was originally named by the Romans as *Septentrionalis Oceanus*, or "Northern Ocean" but also, curiously, went by the Celtic name of *Morimaru*, the "dead sea". The North Sea has, in fact, been shown to have expanses of "dead water" – where fresh water lies on top of salt water, creating difficult conditions for mariners and uninhabitable areas for marine life. Talking of which, the North Sea is home to well over 200 different species of fish and crustaceans including cod, herring, sole, lobster, oysters and mussels as well as a surprisingly large variety of marine mammals as will be revealed later.

All this information provided me with my first problem. At the mouth of a river, and at the Humber Estuary in particular, where does water stop being in the river and start being in the sea? Where does a coastline become a riverbank? Time for some more specific research…

I soon learned that the Humber is considered to be a tidal estuary AND that it is on the East Coast of England, but that the same area is marked on Ordnance Maps as the River Humber. So what about a bit of practical common sense instead?

Lines are usually straight aren't they? So I could apply the principle to a coastline. What if I drew a straight line from, say, Spurn Point to Cleethorpes? That would give a pretty continuous straight coastline to follow. But then, the ports of Grimsby and Hull would not be considered as coastal. That felt wrong to me.

Considering Hull actually led me to an answer that I was satisfied with. I found several articles about the Port of Hull that referred to its location at the confluence of the Humber River and Humber Estuary. I could use Hull as a coastline terminus as well as one for shipping!

So, now I had a southern end for my tour of the Yorkshire coast. But what about the northern limits?

As a child I remember listening to countless shipping forecasts for mystical places with names such as *German Bight* (which, as my Dad always reminded me, used to be known as *Heligoland*), *Forties, Viking, Cromarty* and *Rockall*. Perhaps a map of the shipping areas might help? Sadly, no. Withernsea is definitely in Yorkshire, but is part of the Humber shipping area and Whitby is certainly in Yorkshire but falls within the Tyne shipping zone. Prior to 1948, the situation was even less helpful. In those days, the Humber shipping area stretched all the way from Yarmouth to Berwick.

No, much as I would have liked the shipping forecast to come to my rescue, it isn't going to help me on this occasion.

The problem now becomes one of land counties not coastlines. Where is Yorkshire? Where does it begin and end? This is a thorny issue in many ways. Local Government boundary reorganisations happen frequently – some places apparently disappear overnight. Thank goodness we don't need to consider Salop or Rutland for example. We do need to address Cleveland in this regard. Take the tiny village of Staithes north of Whitby. Look at any map of the North York Moors National Park and there it is, the most northerly point. But look at a map of Cleveland and there it is too, the most Easterly point. It doesn't really help matters that a bistro in the village by the name of Cleveland Corner has a postal address in North Yorkshire.

Thank goodness for The Association of British Counties. A careful study of their website (with some fantastic maps too, I might add) clears it all up. The "historic" county of Yorkshire extends to the Tees estuary – and always has. Redcar and Cleveland (to use the correct title) is a Local Authority Borough. In other words, if it is in Cleveland, it is still in Yorkshire too.

Having considered where Yorkshire is, and isn't, perhaps a slight detour is in order to discover how Yorkshire even came about. England's largest county and, as some might say, the traditional home of the English, almost certainly owes its existence to the Vikings. Prior to the Danelaw, the modern county we know as Yorkshire fell entirely within the medieval Anglian kingdom of Northumbria, with Bamburgh, on the North-East coast initially serving as its northern capital, and York fulfilling the corresponding role in the southern part of the kingdom, before taking over full responsibility for the entire kingdom. From the ninth century onwards Norse invaders took increasing control of York (or Jórvík, as it was known at the time). This Danish kingdom covered virtually all of what is now known as Yorkshire. This was a volatile period during which for a time the Kingdom of Wessex built power from the south and Jórvík became part of Northumbria one again. It was only the ascent of the Normans following the rule of William the Conqueror that saw Yorkshire emerge once again as the county we now know it. Richard III did plan to remove Scarborough and the surrounding area from the county, but as will be revealed later, this was thwarted by him being killed before his intentions could be acted upon.

Two of the three Yorkshire Ridings (East and North) border the North Sea, with the West Riding being land-locked. The word "riding" has its ancestry in an Old Norse word meaning "third part", further evidence of the strong Scandinavian influence on the shaping of England's largest county.

So, now you have it. To stand a chance of being included in this guide a location must be somewhere between Middlesbrough and Hull, and at least overlook the sea (or an estuary). Oh, and it must have something really special (substitute amazing/beautiful/unique/bizarre) about it that made me want to share it with you.

Of course, this point means that we could still fall out. There are only 26 letters in the alphabet, and I decided to restrict this guide to 50 entries to keep the size, cost and number of maps reasonable. As a result, you may not always agree with the places I have chosen to feature or the reasons for featuring them. For example, Filey gets several mentions but I have not selected the very beautiful Filey Dams Nature Reserve – a managed freshwater marsh the size of about 5 athletics stadiums, and a must visit venue for wildlife lovers. There simply wasn't enough space for everything – this time around. The unavoidable fact is that the Yorkshire coastline as used in this guide is in excess of 100 miles long so I just can't possibly cover it all in one relatively short book.

By the way, measuring coastlines is something of a dark art. The problem is caused by the fractal-like properties of coastlines. Basically, nothing is ever straight, so it is virtually impossible to measure really accurately. Try this experiment. Take the most detailed map of a coastline you can find – it doesn't matter if it is Yorkshire or some other place. Now take (carefully) a pile of matchsticks and see if you can use them to trace the coastline as closely as possible. Can't be done very well can it? Too many bumps, corners and inlets. OK, so let's try the same map but with a smaller stick. Cut your matchsticks carefully so that you have a big pile of them all exactly 1cm long. Still can't get an accurate fit can you? And that is the problem. At every stage of magnification there will always be little bits that stick out or bob in so cartographers actually do their best to estimate lengths of coastlines. Also, do you measure at high tide, low tide or somewhere in-between. These issues help us to understand why one source will claim the length of the UK coastline to be as much as 19,491 miles, while another reckons it to be as little as 7,723 miles. And we haven't even considered whether offshore islands, rock and stack formations should be included.

Perhaps it should also be mentioned that many hundreds of thousands of the inhabitants of Yorkshire actually live nearer to the West coast than their own county coastline. For example, Keighley, Halifax and Bradford are all much nearer to Blackpool than Scarborough. Ingleton, on the edge of the Yorkshire Dales is a little over 20 miles from Morecambe Bay, but is more than four times as far away from Filey Bay. Yorkshire is big – almost 3 million acres big. Bigger than Jamaica, Cyprus or Lebanon. Yorkshire is the largest English county by some margin. Lincolnshire and Devon take second and third places, but combined are still smaller than Yorkshire.

Furthermore, Yorkshire is just one of twenty English counties with a coastline, yet it boasts three of the thirty-two designated heritage coasts in the whole of England, covering almost half of the Yorkshire coastline. Only Devon and Cornwall have more.

The Yorkshire Coast also has a proud heritage when it comes to science, the arts, politics, culture and engineering. There isn't room to name all of them in this guide, but here are just a few. Sir George Cayley, aeronautical pioneer hailed from Scarborough. William Wilberforce, politician and campaigner for the abolition of Slavery originated in Hull. Deep Purple and Whitesnake vocalist David Coverdale was born in Saltburn-by-the-Sea. The poet Philip Larkin, although born in Coventry, called Hull his home for most of his life. The literary Sitwells (Edith, Osbert and Sacheverell) all had strong ties with Scarborough. Dame Honor Fell, a pioneer in the fields of cell biology and organ culture was born near Filey. Leo Walmsley, writer, lived in Robin Hood's Bay for several years and based his popular four semi-autobiographical books, the Bramblewick Series, in the fishing village. And, Amy Johnson, much-travelled aviator, as you will read later, had her roots in Hull.

A final sobering thought. In the time it has taken to research and compile this guide (a little over a year) it is estimated that along much of the

Yorkshire coast another 10 to 15 feet will have been lost to erosion. Sections of the Cleveland Way will have fallen into the sea, more homes will have to be abandoned and more concrete blocks will be deposited to prevent traffic from continuing along roads to nowhere as the coastline continues to change. A century from now and several places that I have written about such as East Newton and Kilnsea will no longer exist. Get out and see them all while you can!

How to Use Your Guide

You have three options, dip in and out of each as you please.

Firstly, immediately following these notes you will find an index of locations organised alphabetically. Each one contains a hyperlink to an annotated map. The capital letter in brackets following the place name is the page link to an associated article within the main part of the guide.

For example, the location guide for "Cayton (T)" notes that it is a "thankful village" and points you to the main article under "*T is for Thankful Villages*" as well as linking to an online map, in this case a walking tour of the village and surrounding area.

Secondly, you can follow the topic guide – an alphabetical list, sometimes straightforward, occasionally a little on the cryptic side. For example, "*D is for Dracula in Whitby*" is exactly that, whereas "*B is for Blink and You'll Miss it*" is a short guide to the effects of coastal erosion up and down the Yorkshire coastline.

Finally, you can view this online map that marks all of the locations:

https://www.google.com/maps/d/edit?mid=zR-wiCMof9PQ.kRPr8WAuDWH4&usp=sharing

Whichever way you do it, the guide contains 50 places to visit, organised into 26 sections – one for each letter of the alphabet. Some locations are suited to a brief stopover; others are places where you might spend a week or more. There are walks, cycle routes and drives as well as places to just sit and take things in.

Each map, there are 50 in total, can only be accessed using the links within this guide, it is not available elsewhere, and for obvious reasons, it is a read-only version. However, maps will be updated over time, especially where circumstances such as coastal erosion cause footpaths to be relocated.

Most published trail maps have predefined start and end points. I have tried to avoid this so that you can choose your own route and order of events. This also allows you to build in your own detours, diversions and breaks wherever and whenever you see fit. Furthermore, it enables you to combine features from one section of the guide with another – for example while visiting Scarborough's *Secret Garden* you might also want to take a look at some of the landmarks identified on the *Victorian Town* map.

My recommendations are by no means an exhaustive list. This is a short guide, not an encyclopaedia, so please do not expect each map to show you every single landmark of note. I strongly advise you to supplement what you read and view from me with your own research. My aim is to get you to either visit places you've never been to before, or to see old friends in a new light – that's all.

Why aren't there any photographs in the guide? Two reasons. Firstly, I wanted to keep the price as low as possible. Adding photographs increases the file size considerably and so the price has to reflect that. Secondly, it is a book linked to online maps so presumably you will read it in conjunction with an internet-enabled device such as a smartphone or tablet where a virtually limitless supply of photographs is freely available to you.

A brief word on accessibility. Some places are reached on roads, others on footpaths, disused railway lines, beaches etc. Additionally, some of the venues are in the hands of private owners who will have their own views on accessibility. Furthermore, locations change, often overnight. A clear, flat sandy beach one day can be rough and rocky the next. A wide level clifftop path can overnight be lost completely following a landslip leading to a different (and possibly completely unsuitable) route being necessary. Therefore, I have chosen to make no claims regarding suitability for wheelchair and other disabled users. I hope you will understand why.

And finally, at the end of each section you will find "further reading" possibilities. Please bear in mind that websites change over time and so although each one has been checked (and virus scanned), I cannot accept any responsibility for content, safety etc. As for the book list, my advice is to shop around online. Almost all of the older books are out of copyright and have been digitised. As a result, there is a real goldmine of free-to-read material. Newer books can often be purchased second-hand for a few pence plus postage.

Photography

All photographs contained within the fifty associated maps have been sourced via Wikimedia and attributed accordingly. The book cover photo is from the author's personal collection.

All Text, including within the interactive maps is Copyright © David Leslie 2016

Short extracts from old books/newspapers have been included in the belief that these are no longer protected by copyright. All sources have been acknowledged throughout the text.

Google Maps is a freely available online resource. Purchasers of this book are permitted to access the 51 maps linked to within the book for personal use. Publication of links to the maps without prior consent from the author is not permitted.

Quick A to Z Location Guide

Each location is followed by a capital letter. This tells you which chapter of the guide to read. The hyperlink takes you directly to the interactive map.

Bempton and Buckton (V): Twin villages and Cliffs

https://www.google.com/maps/d/edit?mid=zR-wiCMof9PQ.kvam5OFp7yyM&usp=sharing

Bempton Cliffs (L): The Tolkien Triangle

https://www.google.com/maps/d/edit?mid=zR-wiCMof9PQ.kSh0Fbzy1zWE&usp=sharing

Bempton Cliffs (O): Whale Watching

https://www.google.com/maps/d/edit?mid=zR-wiCMof9PQ.kkSHzojjxQBM&usp=sharing

Bridlington (L): The Brontë Connection

https://www.google.com/maps/d/edit?mid=zR-wiCMof9PQ.kQ_3npVKwsk0&usp=sharing

Bridlington (P): Old and New

https://www.google.com/maps/d/edit?mid=zR-wiCMof9PQ.kwuGSik2vuTo&usp=sharing

Bridlington (O): Whale Watching

https://www.google.com/maps/d/edit?mid=zR-wiCMof9PQ.kkSHzojjxQBM&usp=sharing

Cattersty Sands (S): A Hidden Beach and Nature Reserve

https://www.google.com/maps/d/edit?mid=zR-wiCMof9PQ.k_JJgnQSVvXs&usp=sharing

Cayton (T): A Thankful Village

https://www.google.com/maps/d/edit?mid=zR-wiCMof9PQ.kRjw-pvCKSbU&usp=sharing

Cayton and Bay (H): Village and Coast

https://www.google.com/maps/d/edit?mid=zR-wiCMof9PQ.kePZ4Ay-MntQ&usp=sharing

Cayton Bay (N): Cleveland Way

https://www.google.com/maps/d/edit?mid=zR-wiCMof9PQ.kqPC0m7WREDc&usp=sharing

Cloughton (R): Railway Line Walk

https://www.google.com/maps/d/edit?mid=zR-wiCMof9PQ.kfBmNs9o8GRw&usp=sharing

East Newton (E): Domesday Village

https://www.google.com/maps/d/edit?mid=zR-wiCMof9PQ.khvho8Jz6dGQ&usp=sharing

Filey (L): The Brontë Connection

https://www.google.com/maps/d/edit?mid=zR-wiCMof9PQ.kQ_3npVKwsk0&usp=sharing

Filey (X): The Roman Influence

https://www.google.com/maps/d/edit?mid=zR-wiCMof9PQ.kBJuMdBYPGH8&usp=sharing

Filey (L): The Tolkien Triangle

https://www.google.com/maps/d/edit?mid=zR-wiCMof9PQ.kSh0Fbzy1zWE&usp=sharing

Filey (C): The Crescent

https://www.google.com/maps/d/edit?mid=zR-wiCMof9PQ.kZVsZH8slhyo&usp=sharing

Filey (F): Old and New Town

https://www.google.com/maps/d/edit?mid=zR-wiCMof9PQ.k3KV7kl4c-tg&usp=sharing

https://www.google.com/maps/d/edit?mid=zR-wiCMof9PQ.kDSPuQTf2yP8&usp=sharing

Filey (H): Butlin's

https://www.google.com/maps/d/edit?mid=zR-wiCMof9PQ.kLFkENidlehA&usp=sharing

Filey Brigg (N): Cleveland Way

https://www.google.com/maps/d/edit?mid=zR-wiCMof9PQ.kqPC0m7WREDc&usp=sharing

Filey Brigg (O): Whale Watching

https://www.google.com/maps/d/edit?mid=zR-wiCMof9PQ.kkSHzojjxQBM&usp=sharing

Flamborough (V): Circular tour incorporating the village

https://www.google.com/maps/d/edit?mid=zR-wiCMof9PQ.kk6v-nghPnsc&usp=sharing

Flamborough Head (M): Danes Dyke and Robin Lythe's Hole

https://www.google.com/maps/d/edit?mid=zR-wiCMof9PQ.kXaaKhAl30ik&usp=sharing

Flamborough Head (M): George Fagg the Pirate

https://www.google.com/maps/d/edit?mid=zR-wiCMof9PQ.ketSnv4dbR3E&usp=sharing

Flamborough Head (O): Whale Watching

https://www.google.com/maps/d/edit?mid=zR-wiCMof9PQ.kkSHzojjxQBM&usp=sharing

Hawsker (R): Railway Line Walk (Larpool Viaduct)

https://www.google.com/maps/d/edit?mid=zR-wiCMof9PQ.kZE5b7rf-0xo&usp=sharing

Hedon (Z): Historic Port Landmarks

https://www.google.com/maps/d/edit?mid=zR-wiCMof9PQ.k_4kiiR3XHvE&usp=sharing

Holmpton (S): A Cold War Bunker and a WWII Tragedy

https://www.google.com/maps/d/edit?mid=zR-wiCMof9PQ.kRvgIVc-ws-c&usp=sharing

Hornsea (L): The Brontë Connection

https://www.google.com/maps/d/edit?mid=zR-wiCMof9PQ.kQ_3npVKwsk0&usp=sharing

Hornsea (P): Historical Tour

https://www.google.com/maps/d/edit?mid=zR-wiCMof9PQ.kpOM1CT45GNQ&usp=sharing

Hornsea (W): The Mere

https://www.google.com/maps/d/edit?mid=zR-wiCMof9PQ.kqxYkj_BBbvY&usp=sharing

Hornsea (L): The Tolkien Triangle

https://www.google.com/maps/d/edit?mid=zR-wiCMof9PQ.kSh0Fbzy1zWE&usp=sharing

Hull (L): The Tolkien Triangle

https://www.google.com/maps/d/edit?mid=zR-wiCMof9PQ.kSh0Fbzy1zWE&usp=sharing

Hull (Z): Zeppelin Raids

https://www.google.com/maps/d/edit?mid=zR-wiCMof9PQ.kE_Pee3oT4sc&usp=sharing

Kilnsea (A): Acoustic Mirror, Wetlands and Village

https://www.google.com/maps/d/edit?mid=zR-wiCMof9PQ.kSuDbjqBcWj4&usp=sharing

Kilnsea (L): The Tolkien Triangle

https://www.google.com/maps/d/edit?mid=zR-wiCMof9PQ.kSh0Fbzy1zWE&usp=sharing

Mappleton (B): Erosion Effects

https://www.google.com/maps/d/edit?mid=zR-wiCMof9PQ.kAeb0Pw_ivuQ&usp=sharing

Marske-by-the-Sea (P): Beach Walk and Village

https://www.google.com/maps/d/edit?mid=zR-wiCMof9PQ.ksy2tPKFDeQQ&usp=sharing

Port Mulgrave (N): Cleveland Way

https://www.google.com/maps/d/edit?mid=zR-wiCMof9PQ.kyavBZFtZIDo&usp=sharing

Port Mulgrave (J): Jurassic Trail

https://www.google.com/maps/d/edit?mid=zR-wiCMof9PQ.k3IMAdoblhQ8&usp=sharing

Ravenscar (Y): Alum Industry

https://www.google.com/maps/d/edit?mid=zR-wiCMof9PQ.kXDw4uPaeW0c&usp=sharing

Ravenscar (J): Jurassic Trail

https://www.google.com/maps/d/edit?mid=zR-wiCMof9PQ.krtmRa6mUu_g&usp=sharing

Ravenscar (N): Cleveland Way

https://www.google.com/maps/d/edit?mid=zR-wiCMof9PQ.kZnnB11ZF37A&usp=sharing

Reighton Sands (J): Jurassic Trail

https://www.google.com/maps/d/edit?mid=zR-wiCMof9PQ.kmJ4ZiKCSJMA&usp=sharing

Robin Hood's Bay (N): Cleveland Way

https://www.google.com/maps/d/edit?mid=zR-wiCMof9PQ.kZnnB11ZF37A&usp=sharing

Robin Hood's Bay (U): A guide for visitors

https://www.google.com/maps/d/edit?mid=zR-wiCMof9PQ.kY6jpOSmXJa0&usp=sharing

Robin Hood's Bay (O): Whale Watching

https://www.google.com/maps/d/edit?mid=zR-wiCMof9PQ.kkSHzojjxQBM&usp=sharing

Runswick Bay (J): Jurassic Trail

https://www.google.com/maps/d/edit?mid=zR-wiCMof9PQ.k3IMAdoblhQ8&usp=sharing

Runswick Bay (N): Cleveland Way

https://www.google.com/maps/d/edit?mid=zR-wiCMof9PQ.kyavBZFtZIDo&usp=sharing

Saltburn-by-the-Sea (P): Beach Walk

https://www.google.com/maps/d/edit?mid=zR-wiCMof9PQ.ksy2tPKFDeQQ&usp=sharing

Saltburn-by-the-Sea (N): Cleveland Way

https://www.google.com/maps/d/edit?mid=zR-wiCMof9PQ.kyavBZFtZIDo&usp=sharing

Saltburn-by-the-Sea (I): Smuggling and the "New" town

https://www.google.com/maps/d/edit?mid=zR-wiCMof9PQ.klJNizGH4nyg&usp=sharing

Sandsend (N): Cleveland Way

https://www.google.com/maps/d/edit?mid=zR-wiCMof9PQ.kyavBZFtZlDo&usp=sharing

Scarborough (N): Cleveland Way

https://www.google.com/maps/d/edit?mid=zR-wiCMof9PQ.kqPC0m7WREDc&usp=sharing

https://www.google.com/maps/d/edit?mid=zR-wiCMof9PQ.kZnnB11ZF37A&usp=sharing

Scarborough (U): Oliver's Mount and the Mere

https://www.google.com/maps/d/edit?mid=zR-wiCMof9PQ.kX7lvsfV7Xn8&usp=sharing

Scarborough (R): Railway Line Walk

https://www.google.com/maps/d/edit?mid=zR-wiCMof9PQ.kfBmNs9o8GRw&usp=sharing

Scarborough (Q): Royal Connections

https://www.google.com/maps/d/edit?mid=zR-wiCMof9PQ.kEcoOfYcBQ1k&usp=sharing

Scarborough (S): Secret Garden

https://www.google.com/maps/d/edit?mid=zR-wiCMof9PQ.knLkoGj4jnrw&usp=sharing

Scarborough (L): The Brontë Connection

https://www.google.com/maps/d/edit?mid=zR-wiCMof9PQ.kQ_3npVKwsk0&usp=sharing

Scarborough (H): Victorian Town

https://www.google.com/maps/d/edit?mid=zR-wiCMof9PQ.kSm_cBxZ_cjl&usp=sharing

Scarborough (O): Whale Watching

https://www.google.com/maps/d/edit?mid=zR-wiCMof9PQ.kkSHzojjxQBM&usp=sharing

Scarborough (K): In 1914

https://www.google.com/maps/d/edit?mid=zR-wiCMof9PQ.kbzND9iRsJUU&usp=sharing

Sewerby Hall (V): Gardens, Zoo and Stately Home

https://www.google.com/maps/d/edit?mid=zR-wiCMof9PQ.k1FDWhmu608I&usp=sharing

Skinningrove (N): Cleveland Way

https://www.google.com/maps/d/edit?mid=zR-wiCMof9PQ.kyavBZFtZIDo&usp=sharing

Skinningrove (S): Ironstone Mining and a Merman Legend

https://www.google.com/maps/d/edit?mid=zR-wiCMof9PQ.k_JJgnQSVvXs&usp=sharing

Skipsea (B): Severe Coastal Erosion

https://www.google.com/maps/d/edit?mid=zR-wiCMof9PQ.kAeb0Pw_ivuQ&usp=sharing

Speeton (J): Jurassic Trail

https://www.google.com/maps/d/edit?mid=zR-wiCMof9PQ.kmJ4ZiKCSJMA&usp=sharing

Spurn (G): Trail around the point

https://www.google.com/maps/d/edit?mid=zR-wiCMof9PQ.kagECFgfrHVQ&usp=sharing

Spurn (O): Whale Watching

https://www.google.com/maps/d/edit?mid=zR-wiCMof9PQ.kkSHzojjxQBM&usp=sharing

Staithes (N): Cleveland Way

https://www.google.com/maps/d/edit?mid=zR-wiCMof9PQ.kyavBZFtZIDo&usp=sharing

Staithes (I): Historic Village and Captain Cook

https://www.google.com/maps/d/edit?mid=zR-wiCMof9PQ.k7rw5Pti6d_4&usp=sharing

Staithes (O): Whale Watching

https://www.google.com/maps/d/edit?mid=zR-wiCMof9PQ.kkSHzojjxQBM&usp=sharing

Welwick (W). Saltmarsh Nature Reserve

https://www.google.com/maps/d/edit?mid=zR-wiCMof9PQ.kOlFZQocfrnM&usp=sharing

Whitby (N): Cleveland Way

https://www.google.com/maps/d/edit?mid=zR-wiCMof9PQ.kZnnB11ZF37A&usp=sharing

https://www.google.com/maps/d/edit?mid=zR-wiCMof9PQ.kyavBZFtZIDo&usp=sharing

Whitby (D): Dracula

https://www.google.com/maps/d/edit?mid=zR-wiCMof9PQ.k2CW86SgcxQY&usp=sharing

Whitby (R): Railway Line Walk (Larpool Viaduct)

https://www.google.com/maps/d/edit?mid=zR-wiCMof9PQ.kZE5b7rf-0xo&usp=sharing

Whitby (L): The Lewis Carroll Connection

https://www.google.com/maps/d/edit?mid=zR-wiCMof9PQ.kbewjZQUpNol&usp=sharing

Whitby (O): Whale Watching

https://www.google.com/maps/d/edit?mid=zR-wiCMof9PQ.kkSHzojjxQBM&usp=sharing

Whitby (I): Whaling

https://www.google.com/maps/d/edit?mid=zR-wiCMof9PQ.kTJFErrkfyaM&usp=sharing

Withernsea (R): Railway Line Walk

https://www.google.com/maps/d/edit?mid=zR-wiCMof9PQ.ki8pWCQI076A&usp=sharing

Withernsea (G): Seaside trail, incorporating Greenwich Meridian

https://www.google.com/maps/d/edit?mid=zR-wiCMof9PQ.kzgd5CC1hjzM&usp=sharing

Withernsea (L): The Tolkien Triangle

https://www.google.com/maps/d/edit?mid=zR-wiCMof9PQ.kSh0Fbzy1zWE&usp=sharing

A is for "Acoustic Mirror"

Very few of these concrete World War I relics remain in England and the one at Kilnsea is alongside the Yorkshire Wildlife Trusts newly developed Wetlands Nature Reserve in this peaceful corner of Holderness.

Map 1: Kilnsea and its World War I concrete mirror

https://www.google.com/maps/d/edit?mid=zR-wiCMof9PQ.kSuDbjqBcWj4&usp=sharing

At the time of writing (March 2016) the generic version of Google Maps has not yet been updated so Kilnsea Wetlands Nature Reserve landmarks are shown where they actually are although you cannot yet see them on this map.

For a Yorkshire Wildlife Trust map of the reserve go to:

http://www.ywt.org.uk/reserves/kilnsea-wetlands-nature-reserve

Early in the First World War Britain faced an aerial invasion for the first time in its history (see also Z is for Zeppelins over Hull and Hedon - Reasons 49 and 50). The German Zeppelin Airships flew over the North Sea often unseen until they passed over a town or village.

The military commandeered coastguard lookout stations and built others but even on a clear day these gave a maximum visibility of about 12 miles and the airships were almost impossible to spot. Obviously at night the situation was even worse, although there were reports of night-time raids being spotted as the moonlight reflected off the silver-grey balloon skins. The principles of RADAR (Radio Detection And Ranging) were widely known but not adopted until the Second World War. But what if there was a way to detect airships by listening for them? This is where Sound Mirrors, also known as Acoustic Mirrors served a temporary purpose.

By constructing a concrete parabolic dish facing out to sea and positioning a microphone directly in front it was possible to listen for the drone of the Zeppelin engines as far away as 25 miles. The airships had a maximum speed of around 50 miles per hour so detecting them before they met land could give up to half an hour early warning. Of course, with Hull as the principal target being a little over 20 miles further inland, the incoming raiders would require even longer to reach their intended destination. When atmospheric conditions are taken into consideration, along with the fact that the mirror, although concave was fixed pointing due east, the average detection time was more like 4 or 5 minutes. The sound mirrors main purpose, however, was not to give residents time to seek shelter, but to alert air raid defences nearby at Godwin Battery and further south along the Spurn peninsula, where over 500 men were permanently stationed, primarily to defend the East coast and Humber estuary from marine invaders, but with airships observed crossing the coastline at an altitude of as low as 50 feet you might think that shooting them down would be relatively simple. Unfortunately, not so. The typical cruising altitude of a Zeppelin was between 10,000 and 13,000 feet; so even daytime raids could be completed behind cloud cover more often than not.

The Kilnsea mirror was erected between 1915 and 1916 to serve as an early warning station following air raids on Hull and York. The dish has a diameter of about 15 feet and remains in good workable condition – although you will need to take your own microphone and headphones to check this out for yourself. Initial observation of the mirror might lead you to think of it as a fairly rudimentary structure, which by today's standards it most certainly is, but in World War I, with the ability of an active listener determine a rough bearing of the incoming raiders by moving the microphone to find the position of the loudest noise, it was a genuine lifesaver.

It is a simple question of acoustics. Whenever sound hits a solid object, some of the sound waves are absorbed by the object, some pass through, or become transmitted sounds and the rest are reflected back off the object. Concrete is an ideal material for a sound mirror as it can reflect back up to 97% of all sound that it receives. Also, low frequency sounds, such as those caused by airship engines, are much less likely to be absorbed by a dense material such as concrete. In terms of the science, the only thing Kilnsea's Acoustic Mirror lacked to increase its efficiency was a coat of paint. All in all, concrete acoustic mirrors were a pretty neat idea.

The village of Kilnsea itself was never likely to be an intentional target, although many places were bombed by Zeppelins returning to Germany having aborted missions, but carrying too much weight for the journey home. Even if a Zeppelin commander had ordered bombs to be dropped over Kilnsea, the chances of them hitting a building were remote. Kilnsea is one of those villages where the next-door neighbour might live up to a quarter of a mile away. Kilnsea had changed little since Wilson's *Imperial Gazetteer of England and Wales* described it in the 1870's as:

"a parish … on the coast … Acres: 11,036; of which 10, 026 are water … Population, 179. Houses, 37"

This information helps to explain the old English origin of the name Kilnsea (previously *Kilnese* or even *Chilnesse* in the Domesday Book) – the pool by the kiln. You will read more about the wetlands in this area later in the guide. Perhaps, before proceeding, it should be made clear that Kilnsea as Wilson described it, and as we know it now, is, in fact, the second village to bear the name in the area. Virtually all traces of the first, Old Kilnsea, were lost to the encroaching sea by the middle of the nineteenth century. When the original "Old" Kilnsea church was in danger of imminent collapse in 1826, gravestones were quickly removed and relocated in the northern end of the churchyard at Easington. It is unclear whether all the coffins were moved along with the memorial stones.

One other significant item was salvaged from Old Kilnsea. In 1828, the *York Herald* reported on the condition of the *Kilnsea Cross*, which, the paper said:

"was removed from Kilnsea by the late Sir Thomas Constable, to save it from falling into the sea, is now, by the permission of Sir Clifford Constable, re-erecting at Hedon, in a handsome square formed for the purpose. When, why, or by whom this curious monument was first raised at Kilnsea, neither history nor even tradition gives the slightest information."

Sir Thomas Constable, of Burton Constable, near Hull, had, in fact salvaged the cross in 1818 before erosion caused it to be lost to the sea. What was not known at the time was that the *"venerable pile"* as the newspaper had called it, had been salvaged before. It is believed that the Kilnsea Cross originated from one of the lost towns of Ravenspurn or Ravenser on the Spurn Peninsula. The most likely reason for its erection was to commemorate the arrival of Henry Bolingbroke in 1399 before his military campaign began which led to him becoming King Henry IV later that year.

The siting of the Kilnsea Cross at Hedon was the inspiration of James Iveson who intended it to be the centrepiece for a square of houses to be built and known as Holyrood. In fact, although the cross was installed exactly as Iveson planned, it was nearly sixty years later that a single house was built beside the cross. Holyrood House still stands as a care home to this day, with the Kilnsea Cross safely in situ inside the grounds. (See Z is for Zeppelins over Hull for a guide map to Hedon).

The story of the preservation of Kilnsea's Cross is a good one. The same cannot be said of the acoustic mirrors. Sadly, many of them have been lost to farmland and the ravages of time and the Kilnsea Acoustic Mirrors days are numbered unfortunately. The shoreline is eroding rapidly (see B is for Blink and you'll miss it!) and it is just a matter of time before this interesting relic falls into the sea and crumbles away to nothing.

Other sound mirrors in less precarious positions can still be seen. At Fulwell in Sunderland restoration work has recently been completed on a similarly-sized concave concrete dish built in 1917 following a Zeppelin raid on Sunderland that led to the deaths of over 20 people. Depending on whose boundary lines you accept, Yorkshire does have another sound mirror. Boulby is in the unitary authority of Redcar and Cleveland. Until 1964 it was part of the North Riding of Yorkshire, so that'll do for me. The sound mirror here is about 500 metres away from the cliff tops so is likely to be standing for many years yet, and as a listed structure it cannot be demolished. It was built to provide an early warning of attacks on the Skinningrove Iron Works some 3 miles further north.

To see the largest surviving sound mirrors I'm afraid you'll have to travel beyond Yorkshire. At Denge, near Dungeness in Kent, a 200 foot mirror is one of three still standing. Be warned if you intend visiting, the only public access is by appointment as the mirrors stand on islands in a lake in a flooded gravel pit. The 200-foot mirror has a twin – at Maghtab in Malta, but this is also on a restricted site, so unless you are happy to view it from a distance through a barbed-wire fence you may have to settle for viewing it online.

Acoustic mirrors had a very short useful life – faster aircraft and the invention of radar effectively combined to make these concrete structures redundant but the principle of parabolic microphones is a sound one (forgive the pun) and is still used to this day in household satellite dishes and you may also have observed it to good effect at sporting events where a sound engineer points something looking similar to a satellite dish to capture sounds from the field of play when a microphone cannot be sited near to the action.

Affectionately known locally as *"the only listed building in Kilnsea"*, the acoustic mirror is a well-preserved example of twentieth-century innovation. The technology may be long redundant but so long as it remains standing it has to be worth seeing.

Kilnsea itself (as you will learn elsewhere in the guide) is rather more than *"a few scattered farmhouses"* as the *Yorkshire Evening Post* described it in 1929. To be fair, the newspaper added quite reasonably to its description that Kilnsea is *"a place where one can wander for a day in eerie quiet, without meeting a soul"*. Nowadays, with its wetlands attracting new visitors as well as a steady stream of bird-watchers and holidaymakers, Kilnsea is a lot busier, but if you are looking for a place to find peace and calm, then you could do a lot worse than spend your time in Kilnsea.

Further Reading

http://www.andrewgrantham.co.uk/soundmirrors/

Echoes From the Sky, Richard N Scarth, Hythe Civic Society (1999, reprinted 2014)

Air War over East Yorkshire in World War II, Paul Bright, Flight Recorder Publications Ltd (2005)

Guardians of the Humber: The Humber Defences 1856-1956, J. E. Dorman, Humberside Leisure Services (1990)

http://www.ywt.org.uk/reserves/kilnsea-wetlands-nature-reserve

B is for "Blink and you'll miss it"

Many parts of the Yorkshire Coast are affected by erosion. Some landmarks have already been lost to time while for many others their days are numbered in spite of attempts (some ingenious, others less so) to save them.

Map 2. The fast-disappearing Holderness Coast

https://www.google.com/maps/d/edit?mid=zR-wiCMof9PQ.kAeb0Pw_ivuQ&usp=sharing

In his book "*Walking to Hollywood*" writer and broadcaster Will Self described how he attempted to walk from Flamborough Head to Spurn Head without straying more than six feet from cliff edge or shoreline. His reasoning? If he could achieve this, then in all likelihood it would be a feat never repeated since within a year most, if not all of his route would be lost to erosion.

A map of Roman Britain reveals that 2000 years ago the Holderness coastline was some two and a half miles further to the north east. When you consider that this stretch of coast runs for close on 40 miles that works out at a square mile of land being lost forever every 20 years or so. Thomas Sheppard's excellent, and freely available online, 1912 guide to *The Lost Towns of the Yorkshire Coast* includes a detailed map showing the approximate position of the coastline in Roman times compared with the beginning of the twentieth century. Superimpose todays map and you find that the Flamborough Peninsula was a completely different shape. A little further south where Skipsea is now vulnerable, the map reveals the lost villages of Hyde, Withow and Cleton a mile or more to the east. Under a curious headline of "**REPORT OF THE 'WHAT WILL BECOME OF US' CLUB**", in 1839 the *Bradford Observer* ran a "*long and melancholy*" catalogue of coastal towns and villages no longer in existence:

"*Aldborough Castle and church are gone, Hornsea Beck gone, Hornsea Burton gone, Hyth gone, Withow gone, Birstal Garth and Priory gone, Frisemarisk gone, Outhfleet gone, Saltagh gone, Thurlethorp gone, Withernsea Church gone.*"

Sheppard's Map shows them all. The village of Atwick, two miles north of Hornsea has a cross beside Atwick Hall that has served as a valuable reference point over the years. In 1786, the cross (which is now little more than a stump) was measured at 980 yards from the cliff face. By 1832, the sea was 95 yards nearer and by February 1912 the distance was 705 yards. In total then, 275 yards lost in 125 years – an average of well over 2 yards every year.

One of the best locations to view first-hand the loss of land is the *Blue Bell Café* at Kilnsea near the start of Spurn Point. Originally built as an inn in 1847 a stone was laid into the North wall indicating that the sea was 534 yards away. The *Hull Daily Mail* reported in 1928 that the distance had shrunk to about 300 yards. When the *Blue Bell* was being restored in 1994 surveyors re-measured and a new stone was placed alongside the original bearing the inscription "*190 yards from the sea*". That's a loss of 344 yards (or just over 1000 feet) in 147 years, or just over 7 feet every year. At that rate the *Blue Bell Café* will begin to fall into the sea by 2075, but the car park and public toilets standing between the café and the sea will be gone long before then.

As we have already discovered, many places are already long gone. Further up the coast at Withernsea since the time of King John there had been two churches, known locally as the Sister Kirks. St. Mary's Church in the old village of Withernsea was lost to the sea in the first half of the fifteenth century. Her sister church, at Owthorne lasted until a particularly strong tide on the night of 16th February 1816. Newspapers including the Ipswich Journal reported the demise of the cliff-top chapel stating that "*it had long ceased to be any thing (sic) but a ruin, except a guide to seamen*". Bulmer's 1892 History and Directory of East Yorkshire took up the story:

"*The sea here, as in other parts of the coast of Holderness, is continually encroaching on the land, and places and homesteads mentioned in old deeds now lie under the water. The church, which was known as the*

"Sister Kirk," disappeared within living memory. The sea began to waste the foundations of the churchyard in 1786; and 10 years later the church was dismantled. On the night of the 16th February, 1816, after a storm of unusual violence, a large portion of the eastern end fell, and was washed down the cliffs, and coffins and bodies in various states of preservation were strewn upon the shore. In 1838, there was scarcely a remnant of the churchyard left; and in the spring of 1844, the old parsonage House and two cottages shared the same fate."

Local legend has it that as well as some of the graveyard remains being reinterred in the churchyard at nearby Rimswell, body snatchers came from as far away as London in search of corpses to steal from their coffins.

The village of Mappleton has some good examples of the methods tried over the years to halt the advancing seas. A coastal management scheme initiated in 1991 saw two new defence systems installed. Firstly, the base of the cliff was built up with layers of hard rocks. These provide a physical barrier and absorb much of the tidal energy. The second installation saw two rock groynes spurring out to the sea. Groynes have been built for centuries in an effort to see off the threat from the tides – the remains of several wooden ones can be seen when walking along the Spurn Coast as well as at better preserved examples at Withernsea and Hornsea. The good news for the 50 or so householders at Mappleton is that these two defences appear to be doing the trick. The bad news for residents and landowners south of Mappleton is that the groynes now restrict longshore drift, the effect of which is that erosion rates have increased in these areas.

A tell-tale sign that a location is an erosion hotspot is the presence of myriads of mud balls on the beach. At Skipsea Sands you can usually see these in an abundance. You won't need to get as far as the beach though to tell the scale of the problem – try Green Lane, for example. At the time of writing, back gardens are on the verge of disappearing. Houses and the lane itself are likely to have gone before the end of this decade.

The problem with the land along the Holderness coast is that much of the coastline is little more than boulder clay and till left over from the last ice age it is very easily eroded. Tidal surges nibble and munch away at the base of the clay cliffs and ledges. These crack and fill with water causing the overhangs to slump into the sea at astonishing rates. Add to this the prevailing wind in these parts is a North-Easterly, this means that all tides are pushed onto the shoreline with increased force. Finally, these same winds cause longshore drift which pushes eroded materials south along the coastline.

So in the long-term as communities along the coastline receive more and better sea defence systems these will protect them, but cause further erosion to the south. There is already evidence that some of the Holderness coastal towns and villages are becoming settlements on headlands with bays beginning to form and sweep out beneath them.

Residents of places such as Knipe Point on the northern edge of Cayton Bay will be quick to tell you that erosion doesn't just have serious consequences along the Holderness coast. Knipe Point is a complex issue. It stands at over 200 feet above the sea and at first glance gives the appearance of being a firm rocky headland. Not so. Knipe Point not only gets eaten away by the advancing tides from below, but rainwater seeping steadily through the clay from above also causes regular landslips. Most notably, in recent years, in the Spring of 2008 following a prolonged spell of heavy rain a major landslide led to the enforced demolition of three homes and left several more in precarious positions. Attempts to shore up the cliff from below and to re-route rain water from above have so far proved to be unsuccessful, partly due to the fact that the whole headland is designated a site of Special Scientific Interest and therefore any "structural" alterations require an analysis on the potential impact on the environment, its wildlife and habitat as well as on the preservation of housing.

Even further north, Robin Hood's Bay has had a long history of problems caused by coastal erosion. Prior to 1780, Kings Street was the main access road into the village, but a major landslide took much of the road away as well as several homes. Estimates vary, but it is not an exaggeration to suggest that more buildings have been lost from Robin Hoods Bay over time than remain standing today. And, some of those are at great risk. Take the Victoria Hotel, for example. Standing on Station Road at the top of the hill above the bay, you might think it would be safe from erosion. Unfortunately not. One of the consequences of constructing the tallest concrete sea walls along the East coast to protect the lower part of the village is that erosion of the cliff to the north – directly behind the Victoria Hotel – is now continuing at a faster pace. At present the hotel is losing its gardens slowly but steadily. The road beside the hotel is also threatened and this is the only service route to the lower half of the village.

Some people are clearly trying hard to prevent erosion, but a visit to Staithes will show you how humans can also cause it. At one time, attempts were made to mine the ironstone seam that emerges here. The consequences can be observed by studying photographs taken several decades ago with the landscape now. Where the ironstone has been removed, undercutting the cliff face above it, collapse over time has been an inevitable consequence. A monitoring programme conducted between 2011 and 2014 found that around 1000 cubic metres of rock had fallen from Cowbar alone.

Interestingly, although it is understandably a cause of great distress to all those whose homes and livelihoods are impacted by coastal erosion, it seems that all the analysts draw similar conclusions. Firstly, coastal erosion is inevitable pretty much anywhere and so we should expect to be continually remapping our coastlines. Secondly, if we continue to build so close to places where erosion is known to occur, then we can only expect trouble sooner or later.

Further Reading

For a detailed technical report on the topic of coastal erosion visit:

http://www.bgs.ac.uk/research/climatechange/environment/coastal/coastalErosion.html

The East Riding of Yorkshire, Bernard Hobson, Cambridge University Press (1924 reprinted 2012)

Holderness and the Holdernessians - a few notes, Anonymous (1878)

The Lost Towns of the Yorkshire Coast, Thomas Sheppard, A. Brown & Sons (1912)

Walking to Hollywood, Will Self, Bloomsbury (2010)

C is for "The Crescent at Filey"

The Crescent, Crescent Gardens, Glen Gardens and several associated landmarks adjacent to this clifftop seafront arc have a long history to explore

Map 3: Filey's Victorian (and other) structures overlooking the sea

https://www.google.com/maps/d/edit?mid=zR-wiCMof9PQ.kZVsZH8slhyo&usp=sharing

John Wilkes Unett (1770 – 1856), the son of the Reverend Thomas Unett was a solicitor and founder member of the Birmingham Law Society. He was also a prolific property developer in Smethwick as well as Filey. His brothers George and William both had lengthy periods of military service in the Caribbean and Europe and his son, Lieutenant Colonel Thomas Unett died leading the 19th Regiment – the Green Howards at the battle of the Great Redan, part of the siege of Sebastopol in September 1855 and is buried in St. Oswald's Church graveyard. George, a Major in the Royal Artillery, was at the Battle of Waterloo and later led part of the advance on Paris. It is possible that a visit by John to his brother in occupied Paris in 1815 helped to shape his ideas for what was to become the Crescent at Filey.

A memorial inscription to John Wilkes Unett in the South Transept of St. Oswald's Church described him simply, yet very effectively as:

"the original projector of New Filey"

Between 1835 and 1836 Unett made several land purchases, in total acquiring over 30 acres of prime clifftop building sites running as far back from the coastline as what is now West Avenue. The centrepiece of his planning, realised by his architect friend and colleague Charles Edge, would be a sweeping crescent of tall stucco houses commanding unparalleled views from Filey Brigg to the north, all the way round to

Bempton Cliffs and Flamborough Head to the South. In front of the Crescent would be landscaped gardens cascading down to the promenade and reserved exclusively for occupants of the Crescent and its new hotel. Edge spent three years on his plans, but construction work took another 20 before the project was finally completed. The magnificent Crescent is rather less curved than the original designs specified. The change meant that more homes could be built behind the Crescent in the space running back to West Avenue.

The first phase, under the supervision of Scarborough developer W. E. Woodall numbers 8 to 14 were erected as a single block between 1840 and 1841, in what would end up as the second building from the town end of the Crescent.

Phase two saw the construction of the northernmost block, numbers 1 to 7, completed by Henry Spink in 1851. Until recently, these were all boarding houses often accommodating different generations of the same families year after year.

The centrepiece of Unett's vision was to be the grandest of hotels. When it was formally opened in June 1854 (it had in fact received several paying guests prior to completion) the *Hull Packet* sent a reporter who wrote in a somewhat understated manner that the Crescent Hotel:

"is an establishment that would do credit to any town in the kingdom"

It was in fact a very grand affair with north, south and east facing windows and balconies all commanding spectacular views over what was then known as the German Sea. Built on four storeys plus attics and basements, the hotel could accommodate up to sixty parties of guests as well as their servants and hotel staff in some style. It really was a cosmopolitan scene, obviously Italian styled exterior, heavily French influenced furnishings within the rooms with their Grecian cornices but with walls covered with designs by the celebrated Chelsea manufacturer Messrs Hinchcliff & Co who had won a medal at the Great Exhibition of 1851 for their new method of fixing 25 or more colours to a wallpaper pattern.

In the period from 1801 to 1851 the population of Filey trebled to 1500, and in the following 50 years it doubled again, but many thousands of holidaymakers meant that in the summer months the true population was several thousand more. By 1920, the growth of tourism meant that the Royal Crescent Hotel had remodelled itself to cater for more customers and now had 120 rooms. To make a reservation by telephone required a call to the rather straightforward number of Filey 60.

In 2005, *The Times* newspaper described how Unett's transformation of Filey made it the *"genteel maiden aunt"* of the Yorkshire coast. I'm not sure I would use the same terminology, but I get the writer's sentiments. The Crescent and roads connecting with it attracted a wide variety of residents from decorators to organists, builders to undertakers as well as providing several dozen lodging houses frequented by the wealthy and not-so-wealthy from all over the United Kingdom and overseas.

Unett worked tirelessly on his business projects, dividing his time between them all. He finally retired in 1855 and withdrew to his family home in Leamington Spa where he died a year later at the age of 86. The *Leamington Advertiser* acknowledged his drive when its obituary stated:

> *"he retained nearly to the last full possession of unusually acute mental and vigorous bodily powers, which enabled him to sustain an amount of exertion far beyond the endurance of many younger men."*

Bulmer's 1892 History and Directory of East Yorkshire puts Unett's development of the Crescent clearly in the context of the history of the town:

> *"The town consists of two parts, known as Old and New Filey. The latter, as its name implies, is of recent date, having been almost wholly built within the last fifty years for the accommodation of visitors. It contains several terraces of large and handsome houses. Facing the sea is the Crescent, a row of very elegant buildings delightfully situated on the cliff, and commanding an extensive and beautiful view of coast scenery. Opposite the Crescent are spacious gardens, artistically laid out, and open to the inhabitants of the Crescent."*

The 1868 National Gazetteer of Great Britain and Ireland made specific reference to the impact of recent building work (including the Crescent) on the tourist trade for Filey:

"The new town, consisting of well-built houses, good hotels, shops stocked with every requisite, and a superior class of boarding-houses, is frequented by visitors from all parts of the northern districts of the country, as well as from more remote places; and owing to its facilities for sea-bathing, its chalybeate waters, and its local and surrounding scenery, is rapidly becoming a favourite and thriving watering-place."

The Crescent continued to expand, finally being completed in the 1890's. The Gardens were vigorously marketed as an exclusive venue for residents of the Crescent's many boarding houses and holiday flats. The *Sheffield Daily Telegraph* observed in July 1899 that Filey has *"a very appreciable number of visitors here, although the season is still early"*. In commenting on the regular performances of the Crescent Band, the newspaper suggested that the season could extend to the end of September.

Times and fashions do change. At the start of the last century visitors to Filey were generally happy to pay for entrance to the beautifully landscaped gardens and their assorted pathways in front of the Crescent and down to the sea below. In fact, the *Driffield Times* reported in 1906 that concert and gala ticket sales as well as gate receipts had resulted in an annual profit for the gardens of £60. Plans were even being proposed to build a large permanent concert hall in the centre of the gardens. Within a decade though, the local population were having to chip in from their own pockets to keep the Crescent Gardens business operating at all. In 1913, Captain Henry Henzell Unett (grandson of John), of York, offered to give up the family stake in the Crescent Gardens. He repeated the offer several times before his death in 1916 and in 1920 ownership transferred to the town council. Today, the gardens are cared for by a variety of volunteer groups as well as various council departments and are used for regular band concerts as well as music, food and other festivals throughout the year.

Further Reading

Filey Town Walks, Filey District Civic Society (1988) available to read online at http://content.yudu.com/Library/A1w50z/FileyTownWalks/resources/25.htm

An Historical and Descriptive Guide to Filey, William Smithson Cortis (1861)

Observations on Filey as a Watering Place, EW Pritchard (1856)

D is for Dracula in Whitby

Thousands of people flock to Whitby every year in search of vampires, ghouls and other gothic legends. Here we dig a little into the town's historic association with possibly the most famous of all vampire stories.

Map 4: Whitby Dracula trail

https://www.google.com/maps/d/edit?mid=zR-wiCMof9PQ.k2CW86SgcxQY&usp=sharing

1897 is widely remembered as the year of Queen Victoria's Diamond Jubilee. It is also the year Bram Stoker's iconic novel was first published. Stoker had first visited Whitby seven years earlier and returned several times over the following six years. He worked as director of London's Lyceum Theatre and managed the affairs of Henry Irving, but it was probably his time as a newspaper writer in his home city of Dublin that inspired him to write Dracula as an epistolary novel. With its newspaper cuttings, telegrams, letters, diary entries and ships logs the reader became drawn into Stoker's work of fiction and many believed it to be an account of real events. The name of Dracula is now known throughout the world but the book nearly had a different title. In the 1980's Stokers original manuscript was discovered. On the front was hand-written "THE UN-DEAD".

The seafront area of Whitby contains several places that Stoker refers to in his novel. But he also used his journalistic skills to weave events from Whitby's recent past into his story. In October 1885 the *Whitby Gazette* reported the story of a Russian schooner, the Dmitri:

"When a few hundred yards from the piers she was knocked about considerably the heavy seas, but on crossing the bar the sea calmed a little and she sailed info smooth water. A cheer broke from the spectators on the pier when they saw her in safety. Two pilots were in waiting, and at once gave instructions to those on hoard, but meanwhile the captain not

*realising the necessity of keeping on his steerage, allowed her to fall off
and lowered sail, thus causing the vessel to swing towards the sand on the
east side of the harbour. On seeing this danger the anchors were dropped,
but they found hold and she drifted into Collier Hope and struck the
ground. She proved to be the schooner Dmitry, of Narva, Russia, Captain
Sakki, with crew of seven hands, ballasted with silver sand. During the
night Saturday the seas worked so incessantly upon her that her masts
went by the board and on Sunday morning she lay high and dry a broken
and complete wreck, firmly embedded in the sand."*

In the novel, Stoker describes how Dracula in the form of a dog arrives
aboard the Russian ship *The Demeter* laden with a cargo of crates of
earth. Dracula is the only survivor of the Demeter which was washed up
on the shore following heavy storms. The parallels with the Dmitri are
clear. Stoker's choice of name for the ship is apt. Demeter not only sounds
similar to Dmitri, but in Greek mythology, Demeter, the goddess of corn,
grains and harvests had a daughter, Persephone who was abducted by
Hades to become his wife in the underworld. Choosing a black dog for the
form of Dracula owes much to local legend. Throughout the north of
England, a *barghest* was a monstrous black dog with huge fang teeth that
prowled the dark night streets searching for human prey. In some tales,
the *barghest* was even able to transform into other animals and humans.

Even the name of Dracula was probably found by Stoker whilst visiting
Whitby. Library records show that Stoker carried out extensive research
here. One book that he is known to have borrowed was William
Wilkinson's 1820 *"Account of the Principalities of Wallachia and
Moldavia"*. This book includes a biography of the Wallachian prince, Vlad
the Impaler who also went by the name of Dracula. The library has long
since relocated to newer premises but the original building still exists on
Pier Road as the award-winning Quayside Fish and Chip restaurant.

St. Mary's Church graveyard is a setting in the book but was also used by
Stoker to find names of characters for the story. Some of these names are
listed on the map that accompanies this. If you visit the graveyard do not
mistake the use of the skull and crossbones icon as being an indication of
a pirate grave. It was simply used as a mark by local stonemasons at the
time. Also, you may have seen news reports of graves and remains

41

slipping off the cliff into the sea as a result of erosion. This is true, but some of the graves used were actually empty as the graveyard contained gravestones for many shipmen lost at sea whose bodies were never recovered. In the book, the church and graveyard are described:

"For a moment or two I could see nothing, as the shadow of a cloud obscured St. Mary's Church. Then as the cloud passed I could see the ruins of the Abbey coming into view; and as the edge of a narrow band of light as sharp as a sword-cut moved along, the church and churchyard became gradually visible... It seemed to me as though something dark stood behind the seat where the white figure shone, and bent over it. What it was, whether man or beast, I could not tell."

Much more gripping than Stoker's first published work "The Duties of Clerks of Petty Sessions in Ireland". Stoker combined his work as a writer with that of full-time private secretary to Sir Henry Irving, actor and theatre manager. Irving visited Whitby at least three times, most latterly a few weeks before his death in 1905, when he stayed at the Metropole Hotel on the West Cliff. The widely-held view is that Stoker based his vampiric character on his good friend and business colleague.

Bram Stoker is not the only writer associated with Whitby. Charles Dodgson stayed in the town on several occasions. Under his pen name of Lewis Carroll he wrote Alice in Wonderland and other stories. One writer with a particularly strong affinity for Whitby was the American James Russell Lowell, who, by his own admission, resided here on such a frequent basis that in 1889, two years before his death he wrote in a letter:

"this is my ninth year at Whitby and the place loses none of its charm for me."

Russell cultivated a very productive interest in politics in his later life, such that early in 1880 Rutherford Hayes, 19th President of the United States appointed him Ambassador to the United Kingdom, a role he held until Chester A. Arthur, the 21st president lost power in the Spring of 1885 (the unfortunate, to say the least, 20th president, James Garfield held office for a short time until his assassination in 1881).

Taking a residence in Lowndes Square in fashionable Chelsea, Russell was very active as both political and literary ambassador. He visited Whitby whenever he could, staying often at 3 Wellington Terrace on the West Cliff where he met up with Henry James and George Du Maurier, amongst others. James, it seems, was more attracted to Whitby by the prospect of meeting up with his good friend, than visiting the town itself. In the summer of 1890 when Russell was too ill to cross the Atlantic for his annual August pilgrimage to Whitby James wrote to him *"I have no heart for Whitby on any but your terms"*. Russell died in New England the following year. However, James hid himself been moved to describe Whitby as *"delightful"* three years earlier and had declared himself to be *"very fond of the picturesque place"* in the summer of 1889.

Charles Dickens, Mary Linskill, Wilkie Collins and Elizabeth Gaskell all visited Whitby. Much more recently G. P. Taylor, a former police officer, parish curate and record company promoter who worked with The Sex Pistols and The Stranglers amongst others launched his first novel, *Shadowmancer* in a Whitby Bookshop, whilst still actively involved as a preacher in the area. Coincidentally, Taylor (who no longer preaches, having become such a successful novelist) also wrote text for a book about the Yorkshire Coast.

Whitby is surely one of the most inspiring literary coastal locations in the world.

Further Reading

Dracula, Bram Stoker, Penguin Classics (2004)

Birth of a Legend: Count Dracula, Bram Stoker and Whitby, Paul Chapman, G. H. Smith & Son (2007)

Letters of James Russell Lowell – Part two, Charles Eliot Norton, Kessinger Publishing (2005)

The Yorkshire Coast, Mark Denton, G. P. Taylor, Frances Lincoln (2012)

E is for East Newton and the Domesday Book

The Domesday Book is nearly 1000 years old, is written in medieval Latin and catalogues in excess of 13,000 individual locations. Therefore, it might not be high up on your list of essential reads but its pages give invaluable insights into Yorkshire coastal communities at the time of William the Conqueror. Strictly speaking, what is commonly referred to as The Domesday Book is actually two separate works – "little domesday" covered Essex, Norfolk and Sussex, while "big domesday" dealt with most of the remainder of England and parts of Wales.

Map 5: East Newton Walk

https://www.google.com/maps/d/edit?mid=zR-wiCMof9PQ.khvho8Jz6dGQ&usp=sharing

Drive along the East coast between Hornsea and Withernsea and you may well miss the tiny settlement of East Newton roughly half-way between the two towns. You really should make an effort to find it since it has a history going back nigh on 1000 years but will almost certainly have disappeared completely by the end of this century.

In the winter of 1085-1086 William the Conqueror ordered a survey of his entire kingdom. Of course, this was not designed to satisfy his geographical curiosity. His assessor's duties were to collate a comprehensive guide to the nations landowners and possessions in order to maximise the tax revenue available for the king to collect. The resulting manuscript, the *Libor de Wintonia* (Book of Winchester) went on to become an invaluable guide to the state of much of England in the early part of the last millennium. I say "much of England" since the survey excluded London and Winchester as they were exempt from tax and other parts of England such as Cumberland and Westmorland were missed out as they had not been conquered by William. Durham was exempt as the Bishop of Durham had exclusive rights to taxes within the county. Yorkshire, however was comprehensively covered by the survey. The title of "Domesday Book" became popular 100 years or so later due to the fact that landowners had no right to appeal to the survey's findings or judgements which often overestimated the value of lands in order to charge higher taxes.

So what does the Domesday Book reveal about East Newton? The first thing we find is that the hamlet was part of the manor of Aldbrough within the hundred of Holderness. The lord of the manor was Drogo de la Beuvriere, often known as Drew de Beveres (or even Beavriere). A Flemish mercenary, he had been one of William the Conquerors most skilled and brave men of arms and Holderness, stretching from Bridlington to Hull was his reward. He soon created his own administrative seat, constructing Skipsea Castle, midway between Bridlington and Hornsea. It was not long before he abandoned his manor, tricking King William into lending him money so that he could return to Flanders before the murder of his wife was discovered. He was never seen again.

Odo, the Count of Champagne became the new Lord of Holderness. It is unclear whether William the Conqueror gifted the manor to him or to his wife Adelaide – the king's sister. Either way, His son Stephen of Aumale was, therefore, a nephew of William the Conqueror. This in turn made him a first cousin of William's successor to the throne, William II, often known as William Rufus. Odo formed part of a group conspiring to overthrow William the Conqueror in order to place Stephen on the throne. When this bid failed, the king took Holderness back and imprisoned Odo. Stephen escaped execution as he was in Normandy and inherited the manor of Holderness following the death of William II. Several generations of Aumales inherited East Newton as part of Holderness before it passed into the hands of the Crown once again with the exception of the manor of Aldbrough (which included East Newton). This was taken over by the Ros family of Roos and Helmsley who retained it as part of Roos Manor until the eighteenth century acts of inclosure.

East Newton itself was at one point given by the count of Aumale to his butler, William and was later inherited by Beatrice D'Arcy a distant relative of William the Conqueror. For a while in the fourteenth century some of East Newton was in the care of Nunkeeling Priory over ten miles away to the north. The nuns had undertaken to malt three good bushels of wheat every year so that each nun might have a gallon of ale. It is possible the land at East Newton was farmed to provide the wheat. Beverley Minster also owned farm land at East Newton, possibly for the same reason.

Several acres of woodland were recorded in the Domesday Book. These no longer exist. Whether the trees were removed for farming or heating homes, or whether the wooded area has been lost to the advancing seas is not known.

A total of five smallholdings were surveyed. Measuring farmland was a problematic affair. Surveyors counted the number of ploughs available and estimated the amount of farm land in terms of the number of plough teams needed to maintain the land each year. East Newton was made up of 53 ploughlands but only had 15 ploughs at its disposal. It is likely the larger number was overestimated to increase taxes as mentioned previously. In addition 274 acres of meadow were recorded. Meadow land was not subject to tax so this is probably an accurate estimate.

East Newton does not appear to have grown much over the centuries. The Domesday Book noted 29 villagers. By the 1870's according to John Marius Wilson, the population had increased by two!

Nowadays East Newton is a popular sea-fishing venue

By the way, North Yorkshire has its own East Newton in the Domesday Book, midway between Stonegrave and Helmsley. Most definitely a big brother to our coastal East Newton, this one had 43 villagers a thousand years ago.

And finally, a sobering thought... It is estimated that at the time the Domesday Book was being compiled, parts of the Yorkshire Coastline were as much as two miles further east than they are now (see B is for Blink and You'll Miss it). Villages such as Auburn, Tharlesthorpe and Owthorne are all listed in the book, but all are now lost to the advancing sea.

Further Reading

Domesday Book Yorkshire, John Morris, Phillimore (2005)

Gazetteer: A-Z of Towns, Villages and Hamlets, East Riding of Yorkshire Council (2006)

F is for Filey – Old and New

The town of Filey has two separate but overlapping histories. To tell the story of the ever-popular seaside town it is best to talk of the "old" town and then the "new".

Map 6: a tour of "Old" Filey

https://www.google.com/maps/d/edit?mid=zR-wiCMof9PQ.k3KV7kl4c-tg&usp=sharing

Map 7: a guide to "New" Filey

https://www.google.com/maps/d/edit?mid=zR-wiCMof9PQ.kDSPuQTf2yP8&usp=sharing

Just how old is Filey? The answer is that we cannot be certain but the area was beneath ice until as recently as 14,500 years ago so perhaps we should start here.

Humans settle where they are confident of a reliable supply of food and water as well as having safe shelter. The glaciers had carved out a natural harbour and the melting ice had raised the sea level by at least two metres to fill the newly-shaped bay. Fresh spring drinking water was in abundance along what is now known as Church Ravine. The deposits of clay were rich and fertile – ideal for farming. Trees grew well, providing a sustainable source of building and heating materials. In terms of security, Filey was about as good as you could get. On a cliff top with good views out to sea whilst also being on fairly level ground giving 3 miles or so warning of invaders from inland.

Although the first inhabitants of the Filey area were almost certainly nomadic, we can speculate that people were living in and around Filey at least 3,500 years ago from a single archaeological discovery in July 1834. The *Yorkshire Gazette* reported the news with the headline:

ANCIENT BRITISH SARCOPHAGUS FOUND

At Gristhorpe just a few hundred yards to the north of Filey an ancient tumulus had been opened. The newspaper described the findings:

"there appeared to view the trunk of an oak tree, three feet in diameter, and seven and a half in length, covered with the original bark, except towards the north-end, where rude representation of a human face had been carved through the bark and outer lamina of the wood. Staples were now driven into the ends, and an attempt was made by the aid of blocks and a triangle, to raise the entire trunk, but to the surprise and gratification of all present, it was found, that previously to the interment the tree had been split longitudinally, and excavated, so that the upper half only was raised, and displayed to view an entire human skeleton, immersed in fluid."

Examination of the sarcophagus revealed that the body had been wrapped in deer skins and had been interred with several artefacts including flint arrow-heads, two bodkins a brass spear head and a ring carved from animal horn. This was no wandering hunter-gatherer who died on his travels. This was the grave of a settler, and probably a leader or elder within his group. Here was the first firm evidence of humans living in Filey. The Rotunda Museum in Scarborough has Gristhorpe Man on display alongside other items recovered from his tomb. Recent radiocarbon dating of a thigh bone and tooth has now put his age at 4,000 years while dental analysis has shown him to be a meat eater whose life was spent in the area around Filey. Modern thinking is that he was a warrior chieftain.

Travel forward in time 2000 years and we find indisputable evidence of Roman occupation in and around Filey (see X is for Ten Things the Romans Did for Filey for details). Advance another millennium and Filey is recorded in the Domesday book as a small settlement with no more than 20 villagers. Where they resided is the subject of much speculation but very little archaeological investigation. St. Oswald's Church on the northern side of what is now Church Ravine was built at the end of the twelfth century. Churches have always been built to serve local communities. If the people lived on the southern side of the ravine, surely the church would have been erected there? The first evidence of people inhabiting land to the south of the ravine comes from Elizabethan times. It was the expansion of interest in Filey as a holiday destination that saw the town grow even further south (see C is for The Crescent at Filey for details). So "old" Filey in my guide maps is largely the area to the north of the ravine, while "new" Filey is the town as we know it today on the south side of the ravine.

Having said that, if you cross the ravine by the bridge at the side of St. Oswald's Church, you will find yourself on Church Street, where at least one cottage has a sign above the door indicating a seventeenth century origin. Just around the corner is Filey Museum on Queen Street. The building is actually two seventeenth century cottages, converted internally into a single museum – hence the two front doors. Built into the wall above one of the doors is a plaque dated 1696 and inscribed with the words "the fear of God be in you".

In fact, prior to the nineteenth century Filey was pretty much the area around Queen Street. Michael Fearon's excellent History of Filey includes a photograph of "Old Filey" showing a line of up to a dozen fishermen's cottages opposite the site of Filey Museum. Unfortunately, these were all demolished around fifty years ago. However, on the junction between Church Street and Mitford Street, a single "shrimpers" cottage remains as a standing example of the Filey of old.

The first printed map of Filey in 1788 showed two main streets at right angles to one another, Church Street and Town Street. The former, as you might expect, contained a row of houses running in the direction of the church, whilst the latter is what became known by 1854 as King Street, ultimately becoming Queen Street at a later date. In total, Filey consisted of little more than 50 households. The 1788 map also showed Mitford Street to exist, behind Town Street. Analysts have concluded that the layout of the "old" Filey is consistent with a settlement going back as far as the thirteenth century. Records relating to a Friday market running here in 1221 would appear to support this view.

The traditional Filey industry of long-line fishing kept the whole family busy. Men (and often, boys) worked long, dangerous hours at sea in small, locally-built "cobles". The long lines with several thousand individually baited hooks were prepared on land by the family "flither girls" – wives, daughters and other family relatives all lending a hand gathering and preparing mussels and limpets to use as bait.

Fishing is a dangerous way to earn a living. The history of Filey's fishing heritage is punctuated with tragedy. A walk around the gravestones that surround St. Oswald's Church will quickly reveal several lives lost at sea. But, as one old fisherman was quoted in the *Yorkshire Post* after three young men of Filey died when their coble, Mary was wrecked in December 1896 *"We have our living to get, and many's the time that we have gone off when it is unsafe."*

Walk down onto Coble Landing today and you will probably see a handful of fishing boats, but in modern times it is tourism that provides for many of the folk who like to be known as *Filonians*. Yes, there is a lifeboat station here, and the coastguard lookout remains nearby, but the landing also features ice cream stalls, an amusement arcade, cafes, shops and not one, but two rows of beach huts – all providing much-needed employment for local people.

The promenade is lined with houses, apartments and at least one hotel, almost all of them providing holiday accommodation all year round. Higher up and back into town, for every building housing a permanent resident there seems to be at least one more occupied by temporary guests. Where the shops of Murray Street, John Street and Belle Vue Street once provided goods and services aimed entirely at Filonians, now these are liberally punctuated with tea rooms, gift shops, restaurants, and, of course, fish and chip shops. Some changes are easy to spot, others less so. For example, on Union Street, the façade of a stylish apartment block includes a stone carved with the words "Primitive Methodist" giving away the buildings origins as a chapel serving the Methodist fishermen of Filey until 1975. Opposite, the building housing a bar and restaurant – a popular entertainment venue, began its life as a cinema in 1911. Looking at the size of the building it is both easy to imagine it filled with moviegoers in pre-television times and to see how it failed to make ends meet latterly, culminating in its permanent closure in the 1990's. The only visible exterior sign hinting of the buildings past is the classic trapezoidal canopy that was once personalised week-by-week to promote the latest release.

From time to time, aspects of Filey had change forced upon them. In early 1918 a pair of mysterious, some might say sinister, fires caused much damage. The Methodist church on the corner of Union Street and Station Avenue was the first to be affected as fire broke out in the early hours of Thursday 10th January. The Yorkshire Post carried the story the following day:

"About half past three a fire broke out and spread with great rapidity. The fire brigade was called and assistance was also lent by the military. At five o'clock all hope of saving the church was abandoned, and the firemen concentrated their efforts on preventing the flames spreading to the adjoining property in Union Street."

At the time the fire was thought to have *"originated from the heating apparatus in the cellar"* but suspicions that the fire might have been started deliberately began to circulate. A second fire a few weeks later only added fuel to the rumour-mongers flickering tongues.

On Murray Street, the Victoria Hall was, as the *Sheffield Independent* put it *"the chief place of assemblage in the town"*. It was, until the ground floor was gutted by fire early in the morning of Tuesday 26th March. No arsonist was ever identified and the Victoria Hall never recovered from such extensive damage. The building was demolished later. The church fared somewhat better, but still needed five years of repairs before finally reopening in 1923. Having suffered the rage of fire, brimstone was the next challenge. This came, after a fashion on 7th June 1931. Brimstone, or sulphur, is associated with volcanic eruptions and earthquakes. On this Summer's day, no-one in Filey was anticipating the largest ever recorded earthquake to hit the United Kingdom. At 6.1 on the Richter Scale it was minor in comparison with say the Japanese Tohoku earthquake of 2011, which was recorded to be about 50 times more powerful. Having said that, the Dogger Bank earthquake, 60 miles east of Filey still released as much energy as the *Little Boy* atomic bomb dropped on Hiroshima in 1945. A few cracked ceilings and a twisted church tower was the extent of the suffering in Filey. One resident, whose home was one of the houses perched perilously on the edge of Church Ravine commented to the *Yorkshire Post*:

"thowt t'whole benk 'ad come down"

The same reporter noted that *Bonzo the Seal* had emerged from the water with his nose *"slightly more snubbed"*. *Bonzo* had been found as a stray pup on the beach some years earlier. Having been reared in a concrete pool and hand fed, *Bonzo* grew well, but was reluctant to return to the sea. By the time of the earthquake he was a popular attraction on Coble Landing, being exhibited throughout the summer season for a nominal fee. Apparently he was a real favourite with the children, including the Princess Royal's two sons – George and Gerald (both cousins to Queen Elizabeth II). When he died, aged 14, in August 1940 several newspapers carried the story. The *Yorkshire Evening Post* must have distressed more than a few children with the somewhat blunt headline of **BONZO DEAD**. The *Hull Daily Mail* had a much more sympathetic approach, even adding humour to the obituary by reminding readers of an incident the previous year when a bailiff seeking water rates arrears from *Bonzo's* owner attempted (and failed) to take the thirty stone seal away on a bicycle, apparently with the intention of auctioning the poor animal in order to recover the £20 owed to Filey Council. Thankfully, common sense intervened for once. If you visit Coble Landing nowadays you can see a wooden statue commemorating *Bonzo*, in front of the refreshment kiosks.

Coble Landing is a good example of how Filey has adapted to meet the needs of tourists. At the beginning of the twentieth century, Filey was already a big success as a holiday venue, but there was a big divide between "old" and "new". Visitors stayed and spent their time in "new" Filey, while most of the residents of "old" Filey continued with their traditional methods of earning a living through fishing. Picture postcards of Coble Landing from over a hundred years ago reveal that it was little more than a slipway, a lifeboat station and space for pulling up and storing dozens of wooden fishing cobles. Gradually things changed. Public toilets were added in the 1940's, by the 1960's Baker's bar and café had been built beside the lifeboat station and Corrigan's Amusement Arcade was a popular attraction. Slowly and steadily the fishing cobles disappeared as the landing moved with the times. Walk along Coble Landing now and you'll still see the name of Baker, Corrigans is now Holdsworths and the café has an extra floor on top and is home to at least three distinct businesses. Where the fishing cobles once lined up is now a row of take-aways.

A snippet in the *Yorkshire Post's* edition of Friday 23rd February 1934 helps appreciate why so much of Filey's fishing tradition has been lost in the last hundred years. Fishing is gruelling and dangerous. Running businesses providing for tourists is most definitely not easy, as any chef or hotelier will testify – but you are unlikely to lose your life earning a crust in a restaurant or bed and breakfast establishment. The newspapers stark words said it all:

> *"Yesterday ... the (Filey) cobles spent nine hours searching for fish and their catches realised only 9s (9 shillings = 45p)."*

Filey has a long history and continues to change to meet the economic and social needs of its residents as well as providing for thousands of day trippers and holidaymakers every year. Yet it never seems to change so much as to lose that sense of comfort and homeliness that gives this wonderful little seaside town its charm.

Further Reading

The History of Filey, Michael Fearon, Blackthorn Press (2008)

Gristhorpe Man: a Life and Death in the Bronze Age, Melton, Montgomery & Knusel, Oxbow (2013)

Filey Town Walks, Filey District Civic Society (Revised 1991)

G is for Groynes

Groynes are a common sight along coastlines around the world. Most of them in England are made from wood, but boulder and concrete groynes are also found in several places. Withernsea and the Spurn Peninsula both feature several groynes used with varying degrees of success.

Map 8: Withernsea Trail

https://www.google.com/maps/d/edit?mid=zR-wiCMof9PQ.kzgd5CC1hjzM&usp=sharing

Map 9: Spurn Point Trail

https://www.google.com/maps/d/edit?mid=zR-wiCMof9PQ.kagECFgfrHVQ&usp=sharing

The primary purpose of groynes is to reduce erosion. They do this by interrupting the flow of water, absorbing energy from the tides and restricting the movement of sediment. Positioning groynes is a difficult science. Sand is often deposited upshore, creating longer, deeper beaches, whilst erosion is often found to worsen downshore of the groynes. Where groynes are not high enough or do not reach out to sea far enough they may be totally ineffective, but where they are too high or too long they tend to make erosion worse beyond the area of the groynes because they retain too much sediment. On the Holderness coast the tidal current flow is from north to south, so any additional erosion as a result of the poor placement of groynes tends to be to the south of the groynes.

At Withernsea, coastal management systems including groynes have successfully defended the town from further seafront erosion. The tourist industry has been helped by the groynes as they have locked in sand creating wider deeper sandy beaches that are steeper than they were before the groynes were installed.

Coastal erosion destroys property, causes loss of fertile farm land and can break lines of communication between coastal communities, all with expensive economic consequences. But coastal management schemes are not cheap. At Mappleton, 10 miles north of Withernsea a coastal management scheme was introduced in 1991. Rock boulders were positioned at the base of the cliffs and two long rock groynes were laid perpendicular to the shoreline. The total bill for the scheme came in at £2 million. The results for Mappleton have been exactly as planners hoped. But, erosion to the south of Mappleton has increased significantly. Respite for Mappleton may only be temporary, however. As global warming causes sea levels to continue to rise, the impact of the groynes is likely to lessen unless more money can be found.

Coastal management systems on the Holderness coast are effectively converting seafront towns, villages and hamlets into headlands. Over time, to the south of each one, accelerated erosion will carve out wider sweeping bays, totally transforming the shape of the east coast. The position of Spurn Point is already changing. Surveys show that Spurn has actually moved westwards at a steady rate over the last hundred years as sand and grit are eroded from the seaward side and then redeposited on the Humber estuary side. The point at Spurn is actually about a mile and a half north west of its position 1500 years ago.

Spurn is a doomed peninsula. It always has been. In fact, "it" should not be used at all as the peninsula is believed to have a cyclic existence. Every two hundred and fifty years or so, the peninsula is breached at the landward end, converting Spurn into a very low island. The sea then washes the island away, and as it does it deposits the sand and shingle a little further north west creating the "next" Spurn Point in the process. Many observers believe this particular incarnation of the peninsula is nearing the end of its existence, pointing to 2013 and the most severe breach in recent times as their evidence. But, once it has gone, we can be assured that the cycle will start all over again.

The latest version of Spurn is longer than any of its predecessors. This is due to the defences restricting erosion and placing collected sand and shingle onto the point, exaggerating the spoon shape of the peninsula year on year. But, unless serious intervention takes place quickly its days are numbered. The groynes and other defences are rotting and becoming ineffective with the result that the peninsula is now as narrow as three metres across in places. The situation is made more complex by the very large numbers of First and Second World War concrete structural remains that have slipped (in some cases, crashed) onto the beach creating unintentional sea defences, often in locations where they make matters worse. There have been several short-term breaches in recent years. Perhaps the next one will be the last one for this peculiar but captivating piece of land.

Withernsea has a more promising outlook. The present curved sea wall is doing its job well – for the town itself, that is. The earlier straight wall had succumbed to the relentless energy of the tides, whereas the curved wall dissipates the tidal energy more effectively. Mind you, at a cost of over £6 million – nearly £2000 per foot of wall, you would be disappointed if it didn't. The groynes are still busy collecting and retaining sand so that Withernsea has a seafront with over a mile of sweeping sandy beaches. Besides, once you have a strong, permanent sea wall in place with an expansive promenade behind it, you have a man-made, rather than a natural focal point for visitors. In turn, kiosks, fairground rides and other amusements can all be provided to keep people entertained – and add much-needed finances to the local economy. The groynes, in turn, do their bit by breaking up the long beach into separate sections and providing wind shelters on those more breezy days.

There are those that argue against any man-made intervention claiming that groynes and the like desecrate the natural landscape. Well, it cannot be denied that groynes do change the outlook, but, especially those of the wooden variety, weather into their environment so well in my view that after a period of time they blend in and become attractive features that complement and add to the view. In addition, it has to be pointed out that, without them, the natural landscape would have eroded away before too long.

Plans are in place to develop the seafront area at Withernsea. Perhaps, with a bit more than just a passing nod to the successful renovation of Bridlington's promenades, the intention is to create a sculpted landscape, utilising the three existing "garden" areas and featuring regular positioned seating zones, sign/marker posts and the installation of several coin-operated panoramic binoculars – it is the seaside after all! Perhaps the most innovative suggestion is the idea to develop themed night-time markets along a well-lit promenade. Time will tell if these plans come into fruition and if they increase visitor numbers significantly.

Groynes appear to a good short-term solution to the problem of erosion, but their consequences for neighbouring communities can be dire, and, when constructed from wood, their useful life can be counted in tens of years. Some argue that any resistance is futile and that nature should be left to take its own course. I can see their point, but if I lived in a cliff-top house or was losing acres of my farmland year on year I'd want something done about the problem. Still further, I'd hate to see the natural wonder that is Spurn Point lost forever.

Further Reading

The People Along the Sand: The Spurn Peninsula and Kilnsea, a History 1800 – 2000, Jan Crowther, Phillimore & Co (2010)

Withernsea (Pocket Images), Ben Chapman, Nonsuch (2003)

H is for Holidays

Everyone has their own ideas about what makes for an ideal holiday at the seaside. Tastes vary and times change so here are three very different venues offering three very different types of holiday at very different points in recent history.

Map 10: Cayton Bay Trail

https://www.google.com/maps/d/edit?mid=zR-wiCMof9PQ.kePZ4Ay-MntQ&usp=sharing

Map 11: Filey Bay (Butlins) Trail

https://www.google.com/maps/d/edit?mid=zR-wiCMof9PQ.kLFkENidlehA&usp=sharing

Map 12: Victorian Scarborough Trail

https://www.google.com/maps/d/edit?mid=zR-wiCMof9PQ.kSm_cBxZ_cjl&usp=sharing

The modern version of a caravan park holiday is represented by Cayton Bay. To the south, Butlins at Filey takes us back to the heyday of holiday camps in the sixties and seventies, while Scarborough to the north allows us to look back at how people holidayed in Victorian England.

Billy Butlin opened his first holiday camp in Skegness in 1936. He believed families wanted holiday "homes" where they could come and go as they pleased, and not the rigid rules of most guest houses of the period where the norm was to be locked out during the day, whatever the weather. Filey was to be his third holiday camp, but World War II began and the site was commandeered for military use. This was a blow to Billy Butlin's plans but at least the War Ministry paid to complete construction of his site. RAF Hunmanby Moor was home to 6,000 military personnel. In May 1945 as the war in Europe ended, the RAF supported the sites conversion to a holiday camp. By 1946 when the military left, the site was capable of supporting over 10,000 holidaymakers. Right from the outset it was receiving 4,000 paying guests every week.

Billy's business model was simple. Give people somewhere affordable to stay and then provide all the services and leisure facilities that they might need so that every penny they spend goes into the Butlin's coffers. Families did not need their own transport – Butlin arranged for a branch line and station to be constructed. There was even a "road-train" connecting the holiday site to the Filey Holiday Camp Railway Station. For a while people loved it. And why wouldn't they? A boating lake, theatres, cinema, swimming pools, amusement parks all provided on-site entertainment. Nine bars, three dining rooms and two restaurants meant that families could enjoy a day together without worrying about what to cook later. Sports enthusiasts could choose between tennis, bowling, golf or billiards. There were even two churches, hairdressers, a post office and a petrol station provided. Plus, of course, every chalet was situated less than a five-minute walk away from a wide sandy beach.

But it was not to last. The rail service was the first part to decline. As more people travelled by car or took advantage of cheap flights abroad so the railway line became uneconomic. Bobby Butlin took over the business from his father in 1968 and sold it on to the Rank Organisation in 1972. Butlins subsidised the railway for its final five years but it closed for good in 1977. The holiday camp itself peaked in 1975 with 175,000 visitors in a single year but numbers quickly dropped off and Butlins Filey holiday camp was closed for good in 1983.

Did Butlin's help or hinder the town of Filey as a tourist destination? Opinions are divided on the question. Tens of thousands of visitors has to be good for the area doesn't it? Not if they have everything they need on site and don't spend any money in the town? Many of those who stayed at Butlin's never left the site in their entire holiday – why would they, with swimming pools, shows, restaurants, shops and direct access to a wide sandy beach all within a five-minute walk of your holiday chalet?

Billy Butlin, by the way, clearly liked the area himself. A very familiar landmark to all those who know Filey Bay well is the "white house" – a three-storey, flat-roofed art deco building set back from the beach with its own private access. Now it is available, to those who can afford it, as luxury holiday accommodation. Back in the 1940's Billy Butlin called it home.

A Leeds-based property developer, Trevor Guy bought the whole site in 1985 and reopened it in May 1986 as *"Amtree Park"*. The venture had to cope with two crippling issues. Firstly, Guy himself had to contend with a major legal case. Secondly, perhaps, more importantly, the developer's heart never seemed to be in the project. Some said he bought the site with the intention of levelling it and selling it on, while others claimed to have seen plans for luxury apartments, even a helipad to connect the development to the off-shore oil platforms. In spite of an expensive TV advertising campaign and comedian Ernie Wise on board to perform the opening ceremony, the new holiday park failed to attract enough customers to survive the summer season and was closed permanently just six weeks after opening. The boating lake was filled in, fixtures and fittings were auctioned off and the site levelled so that virtually nothing remained. In 2000 a £25 million scheme was announced to develop the site as *"The Bay, Filey"* including up to 300 holiday homes in a landscaped seaside park with lakes, woods and paths as well as swimming pools, shops and a whole host of leisure services – and of course, direct access to the beach. Hmmm, isn't that a familiar design concept?

Just before we proceed, if you are getting all sentimental about the passing of all those old-fashioned "seaside British businesses", perhaps it is worth pointing out that Billy was, in fact, born in South Africa and spent several childhood years in Canada, where the concept of summer camps in well organised facilities was already established. As for all those other traditional British seaside holiday favourites. Candy Floss was American, fish and chips was probably introduced to England from Europe by a Jewish immigrant and the ice cream cone was invented by a Syrian immigrant to the United States. Kites were invented in China, the Frisbee and beach ball in America, even the very concept of a seaside resort dates back to the Romans. Punch and Judy originated in sixteenth-century Italy and sandcastles were known to be built by the ancient Egyptians. Amusement Arcades originated in America, but some of the technology used was French. The knotted handkerchief as a hat was known at the time of the American Civil War. Bingo started life in Italy and then France before finding its way into the United Kingdom. Fortune-telling takes many forms but is invariably traced back to Eastern Europe and Northern India. Still, we did invent the deckchair, right? Not quite. Although an Englishman by the name of Moore did patent and sell a portable folding chair in 1886, he was based in Macclesfield, about as far away from the seaside as you can get, and, folding chairs are known to have been used by the ancient Greeks, Romans and Egyptians. So what are we left with? Sticks of lettered rock (Victorian England), crazy golf (1907, London) and donkey rides (nineteenth century England).

A handful of miles north of Filey, Cayton Bay is also receiving significant investment. This time it is the "caravan" park industry spending money. For some reason, though, neither the site managers or individual property owners seem too keen on using the word "caravan" very often. These are real holiday homes, and for some people they are permanent homes.

The A165 connects Filey with Scarborough. The village of Cayton sits on the landward side of the road, while Cayton Bay is on the seaward side. As you may have read, a section of the road near Knipe Point is actually at risk of being a bit too close to the sea for comfort. Remember, in 2008 a major landslip at Knipe Point led to the sudden, but perhaps inevitable, loss of some homes and others being left in a precarious position. In spite of this, the holiday parks on the other side of the road continue to grow. The thing is, Cayton Bay is a beautiful place. According to census data the population of Cayton village is actually shrinking slowly, but more and more holidaymakers stay here every year. As you pass, whether on foot or on wheels, you cannot fail to observe brown tourist signs pointing out at least five different holiday "villages". Park Resorts own the biggest holiday park at Cayton and have around 500 holiday homes available to rent or buy. The attraction is obvious – why spend thousands every year on a family holiday abroad when you can buy your own holiday home at the seaside with three bedrooms, two bathrooms, a fully equipped kitchen and dining lounge. With change out of £20,000 you can holiday for as long as you like as often as you like, so long as you can pay the annual site management fees. Sites like these have all the leisure facilities a family could wish for and a stunning beach just a five-minute walk away. Cayton has a permanent resident population of under 2,500 but in the summer season when all of the holiday parks are full (and they frequently can be), this figure can more than quadruple. Proof that quality accommodation and good services at a fair price will always attract customers so long as the location is attractive too.

An advert in the *Yorkshire Post* on 21st March 1953 helps to appreciate the differences between holiday caravans then and now. *Trailways* of Leeds were promoting the availability of new *Bluebird Wren* caravans at Cayton Bay for just £169. Apparently *"anyone can afford a caravan"*. Designed to *"sleep four people in comfort"*, the *"lovely model"* was just twelve and a half feet long by Six and a half feet wide. Imagine two double beds placed end to end, and add a foot onto each side – that's your lot! Nowadays, a four-berth holiday home will almost certainly be at least twice as long and twice as wide.

A quick look around at Cayton Bay and you will soon find remnants of several defensive structures erected in times of warfare. Gun emplacements, searchlight platforms and pillboxes can all be seen in varying states of disarray. If you want a detailed analysis of them all, then look no further than William Foot's excellent guide. Of course there are many who see these battle scars as nothing more than severe blots on a beautiful landscape, but it must be remembered that every place with coastal defences also had temporary populations brought in by the military – many of whom returned year after year, generation after generation for family holidays. It's a moot point but it might be argued that two world wars made Cayton Bay a popular holiday destination. Stand on the clifftops, perhaps on the Cleveland Way path as it winds past the bay and it is easy to see why so much effort went into defending it from enemy invasion. The sweeping, almost flat, smooth, wide beach, well away from large centres of population would have been perfect for landing a large attack force safely.

 In Victorian times the concept of a family holiday was unknown to all but the wealthiest. Even if a family could afford to pay to go away employers weren't bound by any obligation to give time off except for religious observance. Scarborough today provides well for holidaymakers on a wide range of budgets. In Victorian times the town worked just as hard to attract tourists, but those who came tended to have plenty in their pockets. Many travelled to the seaside in the belief that the sea air was good for the health and Scarborough had no shortage of that, but the town also had something else that Victorians flocked to take in – Spa water.

An 1853 map of Scarborough shows a "North Well", "South Well" and "Spa Tap" in front of the Crown Hotel and a "Dropping Spring" at the beach end of the People's Gardens as well as more springs on the northern end of the town. The Dropping Spring still flows – out of a lion's head in Valley Gardens, but please do not drink the brown sludge. Scientific analysis has revealed that it is unfit for human consumption. It was almost 350 years ago that a Doctor Robert Witte had first written of the remarkable health-giving properties of Scarborough's spa waters in his 1667 paper "*Vertues of Scarborough Spaw*". Witte vigorously asserted that Scarborough's waters cured vertigo, epilepsy, jaundice and even stopped nightmares. He also informed readers that drinking the waters relieved wind and fostered pregnancy. In what must have made Scarborough's lodging house owners rub their hands together with glee he further stated that to get the full benefits of this remarkable mineral spring water required a stay in Scarborough of at least four weeks, preferably during the summer months. During this time the "patient" needed to drink up to a gallon of the water every morning.

A Dr Belcombe had analysed the waters from the North and South Wells. His account read:

"The first well on descending the steps is the chalybeate water, sometimes called the North-well; and near it the salt or South-well. From both wells the water is perfectly clear, of a bluish cast, sometimes sparkling; has not a very disagreeable taste, or the least unpleasant smell. Although the North-well has been called the chalybeate, it is found not to hold much more iron in solution than the other; but containing much less vitriolated magnesia, it's taste is stronger, or more inky."

Somewhat alarmingly perhaps, the doctor also noted that the water contained an orange or yellow sediment which he identified as a carbonate of lime or iron.

Several different writers (not all with medical backgrounds) published stories of the miraculous effects of the spa waters. William Hunter wrote of his daughter's condition – a nervous asthmatic of some standing, as he put it. Apparently eleven weeks of spa water from the wells plus daily rides on horseback did the trick!

Many claim that Witte single-handedly created Scarborough as a seaside resort but it was Dicky Dickinson who made a successful commercial enterprise out of the towns natural springs. Dickinson, a man who had previously worked as a shoe shiner, rented the site of the wells from the town council in 1698 and gave himself the title "Governor of the Spaw". Needing something to govern, he put up a "Spaw House" with separate facilities for ladies and gentlemen. His business generated considerable income and brought thousands of visitors to Scarborough. Dickinson's Spa lasted until a landslip in December 1737 destroyed it. A newer, grander Spa was built in 1739. This time, the structure would stand the tests of time and become ever more popular. James Schofield described the Spa in 1796 as "a favourite resort for the opulent, the gay, and the infirm". By the 1830's the spa footbridge had been built, connecting the spa buildings with the main town the other side of the valley. A bandstand followed in 1875 as the Spa gradually transformed itself into a centre for entertainment. A fire in 1877 forced the owners into an ambitious expansion and the Grand Hall was the result.

These days, visitors to Scarborough come from all walks of life, but no longer for the apparent medicinal qualities of the spa water. Chemical analysis in the 1930's led to its prohibition when it was found to be unfit for human consumption. Water does still flow from the towns dropping well in Valley Gardens but I wouldn't drink it if I were you.

Scarborough, Cayton Bay and the Bay at Filey all rely heavily on tourism to support their economies. Each has taken a different path to where it finds itself today and each has its own distinct qualities and strengths but what they all have in common is the indisputable attractiveness of a seaside location.

Further Reading

The Billy Butlin Story, Sir Billy Butlin & Peter Dacre, Robson Books (1982)

Butlin's Filey: Thanks for the Memories, Paul Wray, Hutton Press (1992)

Beaches, fields, streets, and hills ... the anti-invasion landscapes of England 1940, William Foot, Council for British Archaeology, (2006)

The Scarborough Album of History and Poetry, John Cole (1825)

The Scarborough Guide (2nd Edition), James Schofield, Thomas Lee & Co. (1796)

I is for Industry

Map 13: A walk around the fishing heritage sites of Staithes

https://www.google.com/maps/d/edit?mid=zR-wiCMof9PQ.k7rw5Pti6d_4&usp=sharing

Map 14: Landmarks associated with Whitby's whaling industry

https://www.google.com/maps/d/edit?mid=zR-wiCMof9PQ.kTJFErrkfyaM&usp=sharing

Map 15: A smuggler's trail around Old Saltburn and the Victorian "new" town

https://www.google.com/maps/d/edit?mid=zR-wiCMof9PQ.klJNizGH4nyg&usp=sharing

Coastal towns and villages invariably have some form of long association with the sea. Staithes, Saltburn and Whitby all developed industries to benefit from the local geography. At the time of the most recent census, Staithes had a population of just over 800 residents. A hundred years ago a fleet of 80 fishing boats was based in the harbour here. Whaling no longer exists anywhere in the United Kingdom, but at what time Whitby was home to more than 50 whaling boats. Smuggling has always gone on pretty much anywhere along the coast – and still does in some places, but Saltburn with its isolated and sheltered beaches was particularly well suited to this industry which for hundreds of years was regarded by many as a legitimate, albeit illegal trade.

In the eighteenth century the fishermen of Staithes spent much of their time at sea fishing for herring. Nowadays, those that go out to sea from Staithes mostly do so in search of lobster and crab in the rocky waters close to the coastline. The Staithes Bonnet is the traditional headwear for women in the village. You are unlikely to find anyone wearing one in the street if you visit the village, but they are still worn occasionally and can be bought locally. A distinctive feature of these linen or cotton bonnets is a quilted or padded top to give protection when carrying baskets of fish. Fishermen usually wore a traditional Gansey sweater. Like most major fishing communities, Staithes has its own Gansey pattern. The Staithes pattern includes horizontal bands of gulls eyes separated by ridges and furrows to represent the fields farmed by the fishermen to supplement both incomes and diets. Having patterns unique to each community meant that in times of disaster, bodies were more easily identified. Like all fishing villages, Staithes has suffered its share of tragedies. In April 1815 the *Leeds Intelligencer* reported:

"On Friday, great alarm was excited on the East Coast by a most dreadful storm's arising just as the fishermen were approaching the shore; not a coble reached the destined haven and all on board were lost. From Staithes, near Whitby, 27 fishermen perished, many of whom have left large families;"

A lifeboat has been stationed at Staithes since about 1866. The crews – almost all of them volunteer fishermen have been responsible for saving countless lives (not strictly true since you can take a look at any lifeboat station website you can read accounts of recent activity including numbers of lives saved) but in 1888 they lost one of their own. On the afternoon of 27th November storm blew in rapidly from the south-east, preventing most of the cobles from returning to shore. Those fishermen that were on land launched the lifeboat and over the next three hours nearly 40 fishing boats and their crews were rescued. In darkness at around 6pm it was discovered that one coble belonging to Thomas Cole was still at sea with a crew of three men. The lifeboat, with a full crew of 12 set out to find it in the gloomy storm. Against the odds the coble was discovered with her crew still on board. These were transferred to the lifeboat which then headed for land. All of a sudden, a solitary giant wave struck and the lifeboat overturned. Twelve of the fifteen men were able to climb back on board the boat which fortunately righted itself immediately. Three of the crew could not be found. Coxswain Charles Horne and crewman Matthew Theaker miraculously managed to swim ashore but crewman John Crooks lost his life when his body struck rocks. He was 41. The lifeboat institution sent his widow a donation of £250 to assist her with the upbringing of their children.

Staithes has literally grown up. Old maps show just a handful of cottages and workshops close to the water but over time, more and more buildings have been added, with the only way being up. As a result, Staithes is full of narrow, winding alleyways and cottages with red-tiled roofs. The beck running through the village leads to the harbour and a myriad of traditional cobles and pleasure boats. With lobster pots dotted about on the seafront it is little wonder that the village is a magnet for artists and photographers.

In 1894 the Derbyshire painter Laura Johnson visited Staithes as a seventeen year old with her friend and fellow art student Harold Knight. The pair eventually married nine years later, by which time they had formed an art colony in the village given the nickname of the *"northern impressionists"* because they took most of their inspiration from the works of the likes of Monet and Renoir. Painting had been in Laura's blood since childhood when her mother accurately forecast "you will be elected to the Royal Academy one day". The prophecy was fulfilled in 1936, seven years after Laura Knight became a Dame Commander of the Order of the British Empire. Staithes was such a profound influence on her work, the artist was moved to write in her autobiography:

"it was there I found myself and what I might do."

The cottage in which Laura and Harold lived and worked is now a holiday home and the Gallery on the High Street features works by the *"Staithes Group"* as well as several contemporary artists.

A little further along the coast Saltburn by the Sea has its own artists group – The *SaltburnArtistsProjects* – whose base is a gallery in the town. The coastline between here and Whitby was a notorious place for smugglers to work in the seventeenth and eighteenth centuries. Saltburn was an ideal location. A small, sheltered harbour. Tall craggy cliffs and inlets either side and plenty of dense woodland in which to offload and hide the smuggled booty. Smuggling in today's world is much the same business – the supply of goods (often counterfeit) at lower prices by avoiding the tax system. Of course, nowadays, levels of supply have increased massively as the huge rises in population has created surges in demand and much of the smuggling trade is linked to organised crime. In

Saltburn at the end of the eighteenth century John Andrew was known as the king of the smugglers.

As seems to be the case with stories of smugglers and pirates no one can be too sure where folk lore ends and truth starts but the story goes that Andrew was a Scot who fell in love with the niece of the landlord of the Ship Inn. Legend has it that he was first seen in Saltburn the morning after Will Harrison, the aforementioned innkeeper, had been found dead. Smuggling was such a part of everyday life that most villagers could be relied upon to assist when new goods arrived. Coded phrases would be used such as *"Jennies coming"* or *"Andrew's cow has calved"* to indicate imminent arrival or delivery respectively.

John Andrew had worked as a stonemason before settling in Saltburn and evidence of his handiwork has been found near the base of Huntcliff where he dug and carved several storage holes for his contraband. Stories abound of secret passages connecting the cliff with the inn and then on to his home, the White House further up the valley, but no evidence has ever been unearthed.

Smuggling was big, big business. Nowadays we have a single tax, VAT, at 20% applied to many goods and other taxes on specific items such as alcoholic drinks and tobacco. In the eighteenth century hundreds of different taxes existed on all sorts of goods from gin to lace, even playing cards and pepper got their own taxes. With tax rates being so high that, for example, the duty alone on a case of brandy would be more than a week's wages, it is little wonder that smugglers had no difficulty in selling on their wares. But don't be fooled into imagining a smuggler as being like a Hollywood-style pirate. Smuggling went on at all levels. In John Andrews's day it is estimated that the East India Company was smuggling up to seven million pounds worth of tea every year in order to evade paying tax to the crown. John Andrew himself was held in high regard in and around Saltburn. It is believed that customs officers used to call on him at the Ship Inn in order to seek advice about smuggling issues. His fate is unclear. It is known that he fathered several children and that one of them also took the name of John. A John Andrew of Saltburn was imprisoned in York Castle in 1827, but which John this was cannot be stated with certainty. As John Senior would have been in his seventies by then, my money is that it was the son. His father died in 1835.

Whitby had its fair share of smuggling stories, but to hear someone in Whitby saying that "*Jenny is coming*" meant the return of a whaler, not a smuggler. The Whitby Whaling Company was founded in 1753 and initially had just two boats. Crewed by local men alongside Dutch sailors their expeditions to the Arctic waters of Greenland were hazardous and not always successful. Still, men queued up to sign on. Yes, many lost their lives and those that didn't return were away from home for months, and in some cases, years at a time, but the pay was good – very good when the ship came home full. Ships generally departed from Whitby in February and March, returning usually any time between June and September depending on the catch. Over a period of 80 years it is estimated that more than 50 ships were actively involved in Whaling out of Whitby and that well over 2,500 whales were caught. The Arctic waters had other wildlife of interest to the whalers – over 25,000 seals were also caught as well as several polar bears. If we take just one ship, the 305-ton *Volunteer* as an example we find from its records that in the ten years from 1804 to 1813, it caught 138 Whales and produced well over 1120 tons of oil. It is little wonder that economists estimated that each whaler added £3,000 to the town's trade every year. Whatever you might think of commercial whaling – the money it brought into the town is largely responsible for Whitby being as it is today.

Masters of whaling ships returning to Whitby were required to report to the Custom House so that duties could be assessed before any cargo was offloaded. The Custom House was initially located at the quayside on St. Ann's Snaith but relocated to a corner position further along the road. A sign on the wall opposite the swing bridge gives away its position. At the peak of the whaling industry the Custom House received annual duties in excess of £10,000. The whalers didn't go without though. A bounty of 40 shillings per ton of whale oil had been in place since the middle of the eighteenth century and boats generally returned to Whitby with the equivalent of at least 30 tons of oil on board. No wonder so many men were prepared to risk their lives.

While the whaling ships were at sea, many homes had to go on without the man of the house – or in some cases "men" as several generations from the same families were often whalers. With crews of up to 50 and as many as 10 boats at sea at a time the 10,000 population of the town was significantly depleted. Not all of them came back either. Out of 58 Whitby owned whaling ships, 16 of them were lost at sea, most of them in icy Arctic waters. One ship, The *James* was reported to have been lifted clear of the sea by the dense pack ice in 1815. Ships that returned safely to Whitby sometimes came home with a bumper "harvest". The Resolution in 1814 under the command of Captain Kearsley caught 28 whales – enough to yield 230 tons of oil.

The name of Scoresby is synonymous with the whaling industry in Whitby. William Scoresby Snr (later Sir William) skippered the *Henrietta*, which in 1787 captured 18 whales. As stocks diminished it was Scoresby who ventured further North. In 1806 he sailed closer to the North Pole than anyone else had ever been. His son, another William was chief mate on that voyage and four years later he took over the master's role on the *Henrietta* from his father. Both father and son retired from whaling in 1823. The younger Scoresby followed a career in the ministry for the remainder of his life, although never in Whitby. His legacy to the shipping industry is a lifelong study of magnetism and compasses. Even at the age of 67 he travelled to Australia in respect of this work. Scoresby published *An Account of the Arctic Regions* in 1820. In this he described several lunar phenomena for the first time. A crater on the visible side of the moon was later named in his honour.

Ships entered and left Whitby for reasons other than whaling. Custom House records show that ships carried coal, timber and weapons as well as agricultural harvests. Even barrels of urine were transported up and down the coast for use in the Alum industry (See Y is for Yorkshire's Alum Industry). The whaling season tended to end in the summer months so vessels were engaged out of season on voyages to the Baltic coast or the Americas. The most successful whaling skippers were also in high demand elsewhere. William Scoresby Senior, for example, is known to have captained the *John*, of Greenock on whaling expeditions from 1811 to 1814. His personal income from the pursuit of whales is estimated at close to £100,000.

So, we have looked at three age-old industries in Yorkshire, one legal, one definitely illegal and one which is now closely regulated but which many wish had never been legal. All three are significant players in the shaping of the communities that now live along the Yorkshire Coastline and for that reason all three are worthy of our attention and closer scrutiny.

Further Reading

An Account of the Arctic Regions, William Scoresby, Cambridge (2011)

Oil Paint & Grease Paint, Laura Knight, Nicholson (1936)

Staithes: Chapters from the History of a Seafaring Town, John Howard, John Howard (2000)

Smuggling on the Yorkshire Coast, Jack Dykes, Dalesman (1978)

J is for Jurassic Coast

If you want to visit a real Jurassic Park you don't need to look any further than Yorkshire. True, Southern England has a World Heritage Site that goes by the name of Jurassic Coast featuring 96 miles and over 180 million years of history. But if you want a similar experience in Yorkshire, the coastline with its rocky cliffs and powerful tides is a timeline for geologists, getting older the further north you go.

Map 16: Middle Jurassic Trail – Port Mulgrave and Runswick Bay

https://www.google.com/maps/d/edit?mid=zR-wiCMof9PQ.k3lMAdoblhQ8&usp=sharing

Map 17: Middle Jurassic Trail – Ravenscar

https://www.google.com/maps/d/edit?mid=zR-wiCMof9PQ.krtmRa6mUu_g&usp=sharing

Map 18: Upper Jurassic Trail – Reighton Sands and Speeton Cliffs

https://www.google.com/maps/d/edit?mid=zR-wiCMof9PQ.kmJ4ZiKCSJMA&usp=sharing

Three distinct, but overlapping periods of the Jurassic period are exposed along the Yorkshire coastline. From Scarborough southwards we can see evidence from the Upper Jurassic period when this section of the coast was beneath a shallow sea with warmer waters than we find today. Faults in the rock layers has pushed older rocks against the gritstone and limestone in places such as Filey and Flamborough, and as the coastline has changed over the past 150 million years, thousands of fossils have been exposed.

Perhaps the most impressive find from this period was the discovery of a largely complete Elasmosaurus skeleton in the clay at Speeton to the south of Filey in 2001 - 2002. An Elasmosaurus was a particularly long-necked plesiosaur dating back some 80 million years. Nigel Armstrong, an amateur enthusiast from Doncaster, was not sure what he had found in 2001 when he found a single tail bone on the beach, but he could see further bones in the clay cliff face. A team of people returned to excavate the site in November 2002 and where immediately overwhelmed by the scale of the task facing them. There were so many bones in the clay wall that removing them singly would have taken too much time and with the ever-present risk of clay walls collapsing on them it was too risky. The solution involved encasing the entire section of clay in a plaster cast supported by wood and hessian and then removing the whole thing as a single block – it weighed close to a ton and a half according to one of the team members, Will Watts from Scarborough Museums Trust.

Mike Marshall of Yorkshire Coast Fossils at Sandsend near Whitby took delivery of the plaster block and spent the following year carefully taking it apart and assembling the many bones into a headless skeleton. Even minus the head, what he put together was unmistakably a long-necked plesiosaur, and a big one at that. The skeleton was nearly fifteen feet long and with its head it would have been well over 20 feet in length. The find was so important that it spurred the owners of Scarborough's Rotunda Museum into an extensive restoration – taking the distinctive domed museum back to its original purpose when it was first built by The Scarborough Philosophical Society in 1829 to a design by famed geologist William Smith. The skeleton is on display at the museum. The town of Filey has marked the discovery by commissioning a wooden plesiosaur sculpture which is located in Glen Gardens. At Speeton cliffs a plaque marks the point where the bones were first discovered.

This area has a long association with fossil collecting. George William Lamplugh (1859 – 1926) is known to have spent much time here camping on the cliffs and then searching along the foreshore while the tide was out. Lamplugh lived in nearby Bridlington where, in his younger days he worked in a merchant's office. He spent as much of his spare time as possible in and around Speeton. In 1884 he travelled to America to study the Rocky Mountains and the glaciers of Alaska. Lamplugh later went on to be elected a Fellow of the Royal Society in 1905. He worked and studied in the Isle of Man, Ireland, Australia, Sweden and South Africa but continued to spend as much time as possible in Yorkshire where many amateur geologists learned from his experience and travels.

Before you read on, it has to be said that fossil hunting is not without dangers. The cliffs along the Yorkshire Coast suffer greatly from erosion, as you may have already read in *B is for Blink and You'll Miss it*. Pulling a rock from a clay wall may bring out more than a fossil and you could find yourself buried in clay and boulders. Also, walking along the cliff tops should be done with real care. Warning signs are there for a reason, and even without signs, dry and cracked pathways indicate that you may be on top of land that isn't going to be there much longer.

Travel further up the coast to Ravenscar, Whitby and a few miles beyond and you'll find examples from the middle Jurassic period. During this time, some 170 million years ago, the sea had receded and much of the area was woodland so here there are examples of land animals and fauna as well as marine specimens. Ravenscar is a little bit awkward to access and fossils are sometimes hard to find here, but this is a good place to collect specimens of ferns, flowers and leaves as well as a wide variety of ammonites and cephalopods. In amongst the shale and gritstone deposits, Jet can sometimes be found here. Jet is the fossilised remains of the Araucaria or Monkey Puzzle tree and is often worked into jewellery. Whitby has several outlets for Jet products and several dozen outlets where you can buy prepared fossils – but shop carefully, not all is what it may first seem. Some of the fossils have been imported (sometimes illegally) and it is not unknown for man-made casts to be sold as fossils. The best dealers will be able to give you full provenance for any item you are interested in purchasing.

Just to the north of Whitby is Sandsend. Here are the remains of an old Alum Quarry where many fossils have been found over the years. These have included the remains of plesiosaurs and ichthyosaurs as well as ammonites such as Hildoceras. The Hildoceras ammonite is named after St. Hilda, the seventh century abbess of Whitby. Local legend had it that St. Hilda turned snakes into stone and that these fossils were the evidence of her miracles. Fossils can still be found at Sandsend but it is what I would call a "high risk/low return" site. Access is tricky and the rocks on the foreshore are slippery and often covered with algae. The area is well-known and has been "plundered" over the decades so it is possible to spend a day here without finding much at all, but then, if you found treasure every time you looked, it wouldn't be so much fun would it?

A much more productive excursion is likely if you travel a little bit further north to Port Mulgrave and Runswick Bay. The Port was home to a nineteenth century ironstone mine and once had its own harbour. Little evidence of the harbour remains as the Royal Engineers set explosives along its length to prevent the Germans from using it as a landing base in World War II. Port Mulgrave formerly went by the name of Rosedale Wyke until Charles Palmer established an Ironstone mine here and realised it would have the same name as another ironstone mine nearby. His answer was to rename the area in honour of the most prominent local landowner of the time.

People have lived and worked in and around Runswick Bay since Roman times, but the medieval village site has long since been lost to the sea. Now a popular holiday destination, Runswick Bay once attracted visitors in search of a cure for whooping cough. To the south of the mile long sandy bay are a series of small cliffs. One of them, Hob Hole was reputedly inhabited by a boggle or hobgoblin who would cure whooping cough in children in response to this verse being sung:

Hob Hole Hob!

My bairns gettin' t' kink-cough

Tak't off, tak't off!

Legend has it that it was only the local women who dared to enter the cave with their sick children. Fishermen have always been a superstitious lot, but apparently none would go in to see the boggle. The eighteenth century women of Runswick Bay were an industrious lot and also managed to build the Methodist chapel which still stands in the village beside the water spring.

Much of the original village was lost in a calamitous landslip in the seventeenth century. Structural damage is an ever-present risk, but sea defences now protect this tiny precarious village. At the opposite end of the bay are the towering cliffs of Kettleness. These are exposed to the sea at all times. The constant battering leaves shale, clay and boulders on the shoreline – a treasure trove for fossil hunters. George Young in his 1824 guide book to *"Whitby and its Environs"* retold a cautionary tale warning of the dangers from the fragile cliffs in these parts. Apparently, some fifteen years earlier two sisters by the name of Grundy were sitting beneath cliffs to the west of Staithes when

"a splinter, which by striking against a ledge had acquired a rotatory motion, fell from the cliff, and hitting one of the girls on the hinder part of the neck, severed her head from her body in a moment, and the head rolled to a considerable distance."

The oldest fossils are to be found at the northern end of the Yorkshire coastline. At Saltburn-by-the-Sea and Staithes, for example, 200 million years ago these places would have lain beneath the early Jurassic ocean. As a result some excellent examples of early Jurassic marine life can be found in abundance. Saltburn possibly owes its existence to the presence of fossils on the seashore. Henry Pease, a Quaker from Darlington, used to bring his children to the beach at what we now call Old Saltburn, where they would spend many happy hours looking for ammonites and other fossils. Pease went on to be the driving force behind the development of Saltburn as a Victorian "new town" – see the map that accompanies Reason 15 for details.

Staithes village is a good site for parents wishing to emulate the Pease family and their Victorian fossil searches. Ammonites and other fossils can often be picked up just by strolling along the beach here, but the best times to visit are following stormy weather when "new" fossils have been exposed and then broken off the cliff walls. In 1968, parts of an Ichthyosaur were found at Staithes and Plesiosaur bones were found when Alum was being mined here.

A visit to Staithes may not yield dinosaur bones, but a common find in these parts are *"Devil's Toenails"*. These are fossilised bivalves that get their name from a resemblance with curled gnarled toenails. In Scotland these are known as *Clach Crubain* which means "crouching shell" and were once believed to heal arthritic conditions. In England the superstition was that these fossils were actually the discarded toenails from the clawed feet of demons or the devil himself.

Wherever you may find yourself on the Yorkshire Coast there is a chance of stumbling across fossils. Be aware that in some places legislation is in place that restricts what you may or may not do with these discoveries and that fossil hunting can be dangerous. If in doubt, photograph and leave alone is probably the wisest choice.

This can only be a whistle-stop tour through a tiny section of the geological history of the Yorkshire coast. If your appetite to learn more has been whetted here are some places you might like to start.

Further Reading

Fossils of the Whitby Coast, Dean Lomax, Siri Scientific Press (2011)

The Yorkshire Coast, P.F. Rawson & J. K. Wright, Geologists' Association Guide No. 34 (2000)

Geology Explained in the Yorkshire Dales and on the Yorkshire Coast, Derek Brumhead, David & Charles (1979)

K is for Kaiser Wilhelm II – "Baby Killer"

Germany had increased its naval power steadily since 1897 when Admiral Alfred Von Tirpitz had successfully argued for a substantial rise in sea defence capability. By 1914 Germany had the second largest navy in the world, but now its emphasis was on attack and the Yorkshire coastline was a major target.

Map 19: Main sites associated with the bombardment of Scarborough

https://www.google.com/maps/d/edit?mid=zR-wiCMof9PQ.kbzND9iRsJUU&usp=sharing

Early in the morning of 16th December 1914, two German battlecruisers positioned a mile or so off the coast began a bombardment of Scarborough that would enrage millions and lead to Winston Churchill, then First Lord of the Admiralty to label the Germans as "Baby Killers of Scarborough".

Scarborough was one of three Northern towns attacked that day. Hartlepool and Whitby being the other two. In all 137 people were killed – most of them civilians. A further 592 people suffered injuries. Of those that lost their lives, 18 were in Scarborough.

Kaiser Wilhelm II picked up the nickname of "baby killer" following a comment made by Churchill. The "baby" was actually fourteen month old John Shields Ryalls who was killed instantly when a shell hit his seafront home. His nanny Bertha McIntyre was at his side and died in the same explosion. A further sixteen civilians died in the bombardment which lasted for nearly an hour and a half. The only target with any apparent possible military connection at the time was the harbour lighthouse. The bombing of civilian homes, shops, churches and schools was deliberate – according to the British press - the intention was to break the hearts and minds of the people with a demonstration of German naval power. Two ships took part in the shelling – *Derfflinger* and *Von der Tann*. A third ship

Kolberg, diverted to the waters off Flamborough Head and laid 100 mines in a line stretching 10 miles out to sea. These would kill countless local fishermen and their children over the following years. One of those was Thaddeus Gilbert, whose trawler *Garmo* had been commissioned to clear the mines off the Scarborough Castle headland. Gilbert's trawler struck one of the mines four days later on the 20th December and he was killed by the blast along with five other men.

Every death was a tragedy, and while the death of the Ryalls baby captured many of the headlines the story of 28-year-old Ada Crow (sometimes spelled as Crowe) also pulled at the heartstrings for all those that read it. Ada worked as a live-in maid at a house on Falsgrave Road while she waited for her fiancé, a soldier, to return from India. The couple had met in Ada's home town of Sheffield and had been apart for over eight years, twice having to postpone their wedding date – once due to war, and a second time because of illness. Ada awoke excitedly on the 16th – her fiancé was finally due home later that day. When the booms of the shells started she reassured her employer, Mary Moorhouse that the noises were probably due to the English fleet gunnery carrying out exercises in the bay. Ada, who had only lived in Scarborough since 1911 was struck by shrapnel and died within a few hours – before Sergeant Sturdy returned.

Several of the funerals were held four days later. Dr William Cosmo Gordon Lang, Archbishop of York attended and gave what the Yorkshire Post called a *"striking address"* in which he described the collective *"indignation at the cruel onslaught upon the peaceable folk of a defenceless town"*. The Archbishop used the word *"indignation"* no fewer than three times in his lengthy address in which he prepared the assembled congregation for the prospect of a lengthy and torrid war with the words *"they should prepare us to steel our hearts for the inevitable sacrifices which a great war demand"*. At the time, many were deeply suspicious of Lang's loyalties following a much publicised reference the previous month to his *"sacred memory"* of Kaiser Wilhelm II when attending the state funeral of Queen Victoria at Windsor in 1901. Unfortunately, his comment was largely all that the press and public remembered from a speech lasting nearly two hours and given (probably unwisely) without reference to notes. Lang went on to become

Archbishop of Canterbury, baptised Princess Elizabeth and played a major part in the abdication of Edward VIII.

One of the funerals was for fifteen year old George Taylor. George was an enthusiastic member of the Boy Scouts movement and had been to see Baden Powell on his visit to Scarborough a week earlier. The young scout had been told that the newspaper would be carrying a report of the Boy Scout movement leader's visit on the 16th, so he got up and went out of his family home on North Street to buy one. As he walked to the shop he got as far as Albion Road where he was hit by shrapnel from an exploding shell and died almost instantly. Boy Scouts did not serve in the forces, they were too young, of course, but they did carry out important ancillary tasks such as assisting in railway stations, acting as coastguard lookouts or running messages. George became the first, and only, boy scout to be killed in the first world war.

In the aftermath of the raids, public opinion hardened against Germany but there was also fierce criticism of the British military response. News emerged that British Intelligence had been aware of a potential German raid for 48 hours but rather than choose to intercept the German fleet, the British navy assembled near Dogger Bank with the intention of attacking the German ships on their way home. The British Government widely publicised the view that the Kaiser had deliberately attacked civilian targets because of his hatred of the British people. Wilhelm was half-English remember, a grandson of Queen Victoria, but some of his public comments led many to believe (almost certainly incorrectly) that he despised his British roots and the British people. The Kaiser had been born with a deformed left arm which, by adulthood, was 6 inches shorter than the right. In 1889 he bitterly commented *"an English doctor killed my father, and an English doctor crippled my arm"*. Clear resentment, but not evidence of racial hatred. In fact the Kaiser visited England several times in his early life.

It was widely known in 1914 that Scarborough, Hartlepool and Whitby were home to three radio stations which were used to keep in constant contact with the naval fleet. Obviously, less well known was that German code books had been captured so it was easy to intercept and decypher their naval communications. Scarborough historian Bob Clarke analysed the pattern of shell sites in 2010 and concluded that the German offensive was designed to target the radio stations and not civilians at all. With the exception of Clarence Gardens and a single house on Queens Parade, all of the shelling was targeted to the south of Scarborough and most of the sites struck lay between the German ships and the Scarborough radio station.

Several people fled from Scarborough, taking trains to the big cities of York and Leeds. *The Yorkshire Post* carried the story of two of these refugees, the Banks sisters, of Vine Cottage, Scarborough who provided *"a graphic description of their experiences"* from their South Cliff home. The first of the shells, just after 8 am had caused the house to "rock like a pack of cards". As the bombardment continued they dressed and prepared to leave as quickly as they could. After a brief respite, the firing continued *"with greater fury"*. When one of the sisters stepped outside to turn the water supply off at the service pipe *"a shell whizzed past my head, and smashed into the drawing room"*. The sisters fled immediately, deciding to leave Scarborough by the first available train. Under normal circumstances the walk to Scarborough Railway Station could be completed in under ten minutes. Thousands were already fleeing on foot away from the station, so the journey was a difficult one, all around them were "wrecked houses". When they reached the station, they found distressing scenes. Only those who could pay for tickets were being allowed to board trains and great crowds were attempting to enter the station platforms. The sisters described helping *"one poor woman"* who did not have the money to buy a ticket before making their escape to York. Apparently, the train returned to Scarborough, following its regular Wednesday afternoon excursion timetable, and carried "huge crowds of York people anxious to see the state of affairs for themselves".

One witness, Mrs. Knaggs, of Falconers Road, was in no doubt as to the intended target, *"they were trying to hit the wireless station"*, she affirmed. After a near-miss blew windows out in her home, she picked up her daughter and sped to the local post office in order to draw out enough money for train tickets to Leeds.

In the aftermath of the attack many local residents recalled a visit to Scarborough in August 1913 from a delegation of German medical workers. Suspicions were raised about the likely motives and origins of these people, who had been warmly welcomed at the time – could they have been German agents on a reconnaissance mission? Certainly there were many who thought it was possible. As the Yorkshire Post reported at the time, it was a very large delegation of

"250 doctors (who will) arrive in a German liner at about 8 o'clock in the morning"

True, as some noted, it was the same time of day as the attack came sixteenth months later, but this was a one-day excursion made by a large delegation attending a much larger and longer congress in London. Besides, at 8 am in August it would be a bright summer morning. When the bombardment came, in December, at that time of day, it would not even be full light. The party even brought an opera singer with them, Marga Neisch, of the Breslau Opera, who performed with an orchestra at the Spa Grand Hall in the afternoon.

We may never know the whole story, but there is no doubt that the naval onslaught of the 16th December 1914 led to a hardening of attitudes for many in Britain. The loss of life was terrible, and thousands of people were directly affected, but indirectly, the propaganda campaign to "Remember Scarborough" affected millions.

Further Reading

Christmas 1914: The First World War at Home and Abroad, John Hudson, The History Press (2014)

Remember Scarborough, Bob Clarke, Amberley Press (2010)

L is for Literature – writers and their works

Many writers have gained inspiration from living and/or working along the Yorkshire Coast. Bram Stoker's gothic creation (see *D is for Dracula and Whitby*) is arguably the one that most people would first bring to mind, but, as we shall see J R R Tolkien and two of the Brontë sisters are amongst several others who for at least parts of their lives called the Yorkshire coastline home.

Map 20: The Brontë family connection with Scarborough, Filey, Bridlington and Hornsea

https://www.google.com/maps/d/edit?mid=zR-wiCMof9PQ.kQ_3npVKwsk0&usp=sharing

Map 21: J R R Tolkien's association with the East Riding at the end of World War I

https://www.google.com/maps/d/edit?mid=zR-wiCMof9PQ.kSh0Fbzy1zWE&usp=sharing

Map 22: Lewis Carroll and Whitby

https://www.google.com/maps/d/edit?mid=zR-wiCMof9PQ.kbewjZQUpNoI&usp=sharing

John Ronald Reuel Tolkien was born in Bloemfontein, in what is now South Africa in 1892 – he could not have been much further away from Yorkshire if he'd wanted to be! His parents Arthur and Mary were both English, with family roots in the Birmingham area, who had travelled to Bloemfontein so that Arthur could take up a senior position with a bank. As a three year old his mother took him to visit relatives in England with his brother. Whilst there they received news that Arthur had died in Bloemfontein. Mary had little option than to remain in the Midlands with her children.

When war broke out in 1914 Tolkien was in the middle of a degree course in English Language and Literature at Exeter College, Oxford. Rather than volunteer for military service he chose to complete his studies first. After graduating in the summer of 1915 he took a commission as a Second Lieutenant in the Lancashire Fusiliers. Following almost a year of training, during which time he married his long-time girlfriend, Edith, he was sent to France in June 1916, but his active service would be short.

By the time he was diagnosed with trench fever in October 1916 many of his battalion comrades were already dead. On 8th November 1916 Tolkien was returned to England for an extended period of treatment. He was far from fit enough to lead men into battle - mentally or physically.

He was destined to spend most of the remainder of the war in Yorkshire alternating between hospital treatment, convalescence and further training. The War Office did make an attempt to return Tolkien to France in the summer of 1918 but commanding officers in Yorkshire deemed him to be unfit. Besides, the battalion he would have led no longer existed having been all but wiped out.

Tolkien was initially treated at Brooklands Hospital in Hull – now a part of the University of Hull. He also spent several months stationed at Thirtle Bridge camp, between Withernsea and Roos and following a second spell at Brooklands, he was stationed at Godwin Battery in Kilnsea at the start of Spurn Point. His young wife Edith travelled to Yorkshire, renting accommodation as close as she could to her fragile husband. As Hornsea was one of these places, the author Phil Mathison has labelled the area bounded by Hornsea in the North, Hull in the West and Spurn Point in the South as *"The Tolkien Triangle"*. Within this zone are many locations that have influenced Tolkien's writings.

The tiny village of Roos is one such example. In 1917 he and Edith *"walked in a wood where hemlock was growing, a sea of white flowers."* Edith danced for her husband in a clearing in what is almost certainly Dents Garth at the southern end of the village. Edith was Tolkien's inspiration for the elf Lúthien Tinúviel whose story is told to Frodo by Aragorn in *The Fellowship of the Ring*. Her romance with Beren is told in the Silmarillion where *"wandering in the summer in the woods of Neldoreth he [Beren] came upon Lúthien, daughter of Thingol and Melian, at a time of evening under moonrise, as she danced upon the unfading grass in the glades beside Esgalduin."* The wood is adjacent to a churchyard where an underground crypt can be found marked with a heraldic stone featuring a raised hand. Tolkien is known to have sketched a very similar design as Beren's heraldic symbol and wrote a story where Beren (who had lost a hand in an encounter with a wolf) had to make his way down stone steps to the underground fortress of Angamandi.

Tolkien underwent several periods of medical treatment during his time in Yorkshire. At Godwin Battery, Kilnsea, he spent some weeks convalescing in the small hospital, within view of the twin lighthouses of Spurn Point. There are some who believe that the nearby village of Easington contains the inspiration for Tolkiens *"Two Towers"* – indeed, Easington has two buildings with towers, but my opinion is that lighthouses were the real inspiration. Meanwhile, Edith rented accommodation at Withernsea for a while. She stayed within sight of the town's iconic inland white lighthouse. At Spurn Point, the lighthouse shone with a deep red light. Perhaps, the most significant evidence is that the older "Smeaton" lighthouse at Spurn had been painted black. Tolkien is known to have studied local history intently, and with a little imagination – something he most definitely was not short of – the two towers, one a beacon of light and good, the second, dark and sinister with the evil red eye of Sauron shining out, suddenly appear. Of course, Tolkien created several towers in his writings, not just two, but his own design for the cover of *The Two Towers* depicts one white and one black.

After the war Tolkien returned to the Yorkshire coast with his wife and young family for two (possibly three) holidays in Filey. Their long vacation in 1922 is known to have not gone down well with the author who described it somewhat unfairly as *"a very nasty little suburban seaside resort".* Perhaps the weather was not good, or his mood was affected by having to take a large batch of examination papers to mark with him. It couldn't have been that bad as they returned in 1925 when an incident on the beach would turn out to inspire Tolkien to write a story that would later be published as *Roverandom*. By this time, the couple had three children, John (8), Michael (4) and one year old Christopher. Michael was particularly attached to a little metal toy dog. One day it was discovered that Michael had lost the black and white treasure. His parents scoured the beach and the rocks at Filey Brigg but the toy dog was never found. Michael was inconsolable. His father made up a story in which a real black and white dog called Rover is turned into a toy dog by a magician. The toy dog is bought by a woman for her son – Boy Two, who then loses the toy on a beach. Another magician restores the toy dog to life. The story continues with further adventures on tall cliffs full of birds (may well be nearby Bempton Cliffs) and a tall white tower (the lighthouse at Flamborough Head is visible from Filey and is tall and white).

Tolkien and his family had a long, but not always totally happy, association with the Yorkshire coast. The same can be said of another family with very strong literary credentials – the Brontë's.

Anne was the youngest member of the Brontë literary dynasty. Her Yorkshire seaside connection stems from a period between 1840 and 1845 when she was employed as governess to the Robinson family at Thorp Green Hall near York. Each year she accompanied the Robinsons and their four children on their month long summer holiday stay in Scarborough.

Just as Tolkien was inspired by the beach at Filey, Anne drew on her experiences at Scarborough for her novel Agnes Grey. A walk along the "smooth wide sands" near the end of the novel is almost certainly based on the wide beach below South Cliff. Similarly, "the edge of the precipice" in the final chapter is most likely based on a view from Scarborough Castle's cliff top walls.

Anne had one final trip to Scarborough in 1849. On this occasion she was accompanied by her sister, Charlotte and her good friend Ellen Nussey. This was no holiday, however. The previous year had seen two family tragedies. Anne's brother Branwell had died in September 1848 closely followed by the death of her sister Emily, the author of Wuthering Heights. Branwell was 31 and Emily just a year younger. Although Branwell's death certificate indicates he was suffering from Marasmus (Bronchitis), he almost certainly had tuberculosis. Emily became unwell shortly after Branwell's death and her succumbed to tuberculosis – a highly infectious and, in those days, often lethal disease. Emily passed away in December 1848. A month later Anne was diagnosed with consumption, the old name for tuberculosis. When Charlotte and Ellen took Anne back to Scarborough in May 1849 the hope was that the fresh sea air and change of scene might boost Anne's health and demeanor and so aid her recovery.

The group arrived in Scarborough on Friday 25th May where they took up residence at Number 2, The Cliff, part of Wood's Lodgings, on St. Nicholas Cliff. The building was demolished so that the Grand Hotel could be erected on the same site, but a blue plaque on the side wall of the hotel marks the spot. On the Saturday Anne took a drive along the beach in a donkey cart, but felt too unwell to attend church the following day. On Monday 28th a doctor attended and broke the news that death was imminent. She lost her life at 2pm that afternoon.

Nowadays, Anne is revered as a literary giant alongside her sisters, but at the time of her death, both of her novels, *Agnes Grey* and *The Tenant of Wildfell Hall* had been published under the masculine pen name of Acton Bell. As a consequence, news of her early demise was not widely reported. The *York Herald* carried this short announcement in its deaths column:

> *"at Scarbro' in her 29th year, Anne, daughter of the Rev. P. Bronte, incumbent of Haworth."*

Every other member of the Brontë family is buried close to the family home in Haworth, but Charlotte took the decision to *"lay the flower where it had fallen"*. St. Mary's Church stands high on the hill above the town, beside Scarborough Castle. Charlotte wanted to lay Anne's body to rest in the graveyard but the church itself was undergoing extensive renovations so Christ Church near to Wood's Lodgings was used for the funeral service on Wednesday 30th May. There was no time for Patrick Brontë, Anne and Charlotte's father, to make the journey from Haworth, so Charlotte and Ellen were the only mourners with the exception of a schoolmistress from Roe Head where both Charlotte and Anne had attended previously.

The grave attracts thousands of pilgrims from all over the world every year. Charlotte returned to it in 1852 to find the inscription contained several errors. She arranged for them to be corrected but the gravestone still reads that Anne was 28 years old when, in fact, she was a year older.

The Brontë Society laid a new stone in front of the badly-eroded original in 2013.

Charlotte could not bear to stay in Scarborough after Anne's death. Her father, unlike many villagers in Haworth, respected Charlotte for her decision to bury Anne in Scarborough and knew how much events of the previous nine months had taken out of her. Patrick urged Charlotte to remain by the coast and rest. She and Ellen moved a few miles down the road to Filey after the funeral where they spent three weeks at Cliff House on Belle Vue Street. A grand corner location, built in 1824, the house had spectacular sea views at a time when much of The Crescent had yet to be built. Charlotte found Filey to be very much to her liking – in a letter written on 13th June 1849 she described it as *"a small place with a wild rocky coast – its sea is very blue – its cliffs are very white – its sands very solitary – it suits Ellen and myself better than Scarborough"*.

But Charlotte had to return to Haworth eventually. She chose to spend a final week in the company of the Hudson family at their Easton farmhouse just outside Bridlington (or Burlington as it was then known). Charlotte and Ellen had fond memories of Easton, having stayed there together ten years earlier. For Charlotte, the holiday in 1839 had given her a first view of the sea when she and Ellen had walked beside the Gypsey Race as it wound its path eastwards towards the small harbour and the German Ocean. The sight of the sea had been too much for the young Charlotte who had been reduced to tears as emotion overcame her.

The 1839 visit had been at the recommendation of Charlotte's friend Mary Taylor. Before travelling, Mary gave Charlotte a pair of embroidered gloves, which doubled as a rudimentary guide to the area that Mary knew so well. Charlotte added to the map during her own holiday. Bessingby Hill, from where Charlotte's first sighting of an ocean had been so overwhelming, and Easton House, her temporary seaside home. The gloves are sometimes featured as display pieces in the Haworth Parsonage.

Bridlington held strong memories for Charlotte and Ellen. At one time the pair of young ladies had plans to open a school together there but like Anne and Emily, the urge to write was stronger than any other urge and by 1847 was already a successful author. Jane Eyre was published in September of that year and became immediately very popular.

Filey Brigg is likely to have been the *"black and rough"* reef described by Charlotte in Chapter 32 of her second published work, *Shirley*. Whilst staying at Cliff House in June 1849 she wrote to her father describing Filey *Bridge* (what we now know as the Brigg) as a *"black desolate reef of rocks"*. During her month-long stay during May and June of 1852 she attempted to *"trudge"* to the Brigg only to be *"frightened back by two cows"*.

Charlotte had one final visit to the Yorkshire coast in the summer of 1853 at the invitation of an old friend Margaret Wooler, spending a week at Hornsea. She stayed at 96 Newbigin, one of the houses that formed Swiss Terrace, halfway between the sea and the mere. In a letter to Miss Wooler on her return to Haworth she wrote fondly of her time at Hornsea, walking on the sands and around the lake.

Hornsea has two other literary connections. Winifred Holtby stayed there in 1935 whilst writing *South Riding*. The invented seaside town of Kiplington is a cocktail of Hornsea and nearby Withernsea with a liberal sprinkling of artistic license. Wing Commander Reg Simms owned White Cottage in Eastgate, Hornsea and T.E. Lawrence (of Arabia!) spent several weekends there whilst stationed at Bridlington.

I cannot end this literary safari without mentioning Lewis Carroll. Born Charles Lutwidge Dodgson in Cheshire, he visited Whitby on several occasions firstly in 1854 as a member of a party of students and Staff from Christ Church College, Oxford, where like his father before him Charles studied and taught mathematics. He wrote satirical poems that summer, two of which were published anonymously by the Whitby Gazette on 31st August. Charles did not wish to use his real name as the university had funded the trip as a reading and research visit so he gave the newspapers the initials B. B. his first poem, *The Lady of the Ladle* makes a couple of references to specific locations in Whitby, whilst the second, *Coronach*, a lament for the dead, begins by naming the town itself and using the name Hilda:

"SHE is gone by the Hilda, She is lost unto Whitby,

And her name is Matilda, Which my heart it was smit by;"

Hilda is likely to be a fictitious ship. At least one ship with that name was known to use Whitby harbour, but that was nearly sixty years earlier. It could instead be a reference to St. Hilda and the Abbey atop the East Cliff.

Dodgson is known to have stayed at Number 5 East Terrace on the West Cliff at least six times. Whether he had the same room on each occasion is a matter of debate, but he wrote of the sea views from his window which does narrow the options down a bit. The building is now a hotel – *La Rosa* and is marked with a blue plaque.

It was during his first visit to Whitby that others began to realise his strengths as a storyteller. A companion from Christ Church, Thomas Fowler noted *"Dodgson used to sit on a rock on the beach, telling stories to a circle of eager young listeners"*. Many believe that he not only rehearsed some of his Alice adventures on such audiences, but that events in Whitby also motivated him to invent some of the stories themselves.

On one occasion, Charles was asked to assist with the organisation and management of a large children's tea party in the grounds of Whitby Abbey. It is possible to make several connections between the real events that surrounded the picnic and scenes from Alice in Wonderland. The *"eat-me"* cakes are reminiscent of the currant bread buns served at the picnic, the Caucus Race in Alice was possibly inspired by races and prizes given out to the children at the picnic. There was even a rain storm that interrupted the picnic. Did this become the *"pool of tears"* shed by Alice in the second chapter of the book?

Lewis Carroll, The Brontë Sisters and J R R Tolkien all had strong connections with the Yorkshire Coast, but were by no means the only writers with an affinity for a coastline that continues to attract the best literary minds to this day. The enigmatic Sitwell siblings – Edith, Osbert and Sacheverell all spent parts of their lives in Scarborough. Similarly, Susan Hill, author of the gothic horror novel *The Woman in Black*, amongst others spent her childhood in the same town. Winifred Holtby, most famous for creating a fictional *South Riding*, based on her experience of the East Riding where she had spent much of her childhood, had a very short life. In fact, she died at just 37, before South Riding could be published. She is buried in the village of Rudston where she grew up, five miles west of Bridlington.

Many are drawn to the Yorkshire Coast in the hope of some quality rest and recuperation time, but there is no doubt that for many, especially those with creativity in their souls this marvellous coastline is a source of inspiration, and always will be.

Further Reading

Tolkien and the Great War, John Garth, Harper Collins (2011)

J R R Tolkien: A Biography, Humphrey Carpenter, Houghton Mifflin Harcourt (2014)

Tolkien in East Yorkshire: 1917 – 1918, Phil Mathison, Dead Good Publications (2012)

Charlotte Brontë on the East Yorkshire Coast, F R Pearson, East Yorkshire Local History Society (1957)

Charlotte Brontë: The Novelist's Visits to Bridlington, Scarborough, Filey and Hornsea, Kevin Berry, Highgate (1990)

Beside the Sea: Lewis Carroll in Whitby, Alan Whitworth, Hollow Tree Books (2011)

Lewis Carroll: The Man and his Circle, Edward Wakeling, Tauris (2014)

M is for "Myths and Legends"

Hundreds of legends exist up and down the Yorkshire coastline. Some are firmly based on fact, while others have somewhat shakier foundations. Here we examine a few and unearth several facts and quite a lot of fiction.

Map 23: Places near Flamborough Head that aren't always what their names suggest

https://www.google.com/maps/d/edit?mid=zR-wiCMof9PQ.kXaaKhAl30ik&usp=sharing

Map 24: The hunt for *"pirate"* George Fagg

https://www.google.com/maps/d/edit?mid=zR-wiCMof9PQ.ketSnv4dbR3E&usp=sharing

Danes Dyke is most definitely an earthwork with a man-made ditch. The problem with its name is that it just wasn't made by any Danes – it is much older. In fact some archeologists now confidently date its construction to the Bronze Age, some two to three thousand years before any Danes arrived in Yorkshire in numbers. Others date it as being a little more recently – in the time of the iron age.

What can be said about it with great confidence is that it is an amazing feat of construction from an age where there was no mechanisation and the only tools were the most basic type wielded by hand. The earthwork is two and a half miles long, running in a roughly north-south direction from Cat Nab close to the RSPB site at Bempton Cliffs, North of Flamborough Head, to a point roughly midway between the RNLI Flamborough Lifeboat Station and Sewerby Hall to the South, bisecting the road connecting the villages of Flamborough and Marton on the way.

The structure itself is not complicated. A ditch was dug, and the bank or mound beside it was made from layers of the excavated earth combined with compacted rubble, boulders and chalk. The bank was then finished with a flattened top layer of turf. It is interesting to note that the construction is such that it defends people to the East from intruders coming from the West – it was not built to protect against invaders from the sea.

The Flamborough peninsula is naturally defended to the North, South and East by tall cliffs. The Southern end of the Dyke runs into a steep natural ravine running down to the sea, which perhaps gave the people who built it a source of inspiration.

Over the centuries Danes Dyke has become densely wooded – the ditch captures water well and the mound drains well and its mixture of earth, rocks and chalk binds and holds roots as well as any hillside in England.

The area has drawn visitors seeking a quieter seaside location for close on two centuries. As long ago as 1831 Danes Dyke Farm was advertising "DESIRABLE SUMMER LODGINGS", suitable for *a genteel family* in premises commanding *a fine view of the German Ocean and Bridlington Bay*. By the 1850's day trippers from Hull were regular visitors to Danes Dyke where the *ancient rustic games of England were freely indulged in* and *innumerable picnics were formed* as the *Hull Packet* reported in August 1857.

In the latter part of the nineteenth century the southern end of Danes Dyke took on a very different appearance. Charles Cottrell Dormer built a substantial manor house some 300 yards north of the southern end of the dyke. Work was completed in 1873. Charles passed away the following year at the family home in Oxfordshire at which point the Yorkshire house and grounds were inherited by his widow Frances. The Manor of Flamborough was already in the hands of her family – Frances had been born a Strickland and it was this Boynton family that had purchased the manor some 200 years earlier.

Bulmer's *History and Directory of East Yorkshire* (1892) tells how the Strickland name became connected with the area with its description of a memorial within St. Oswald's Church, Flamborough:

"at the east end of the south aisle, is a mural monument to the memory of "that learned, and not less pious, gentleman, Walter Strickland, Esq., who

was born at Boynton, in 1583, and died in 1621." He married Ann, sole daughter and heiress of Sir Charles Morgan, Bart., "but had no issue by her; yet such was her love to his worth that she freely gave £2,000 for his purchase of the lordship of Flamborough."

Frances Cottrell Dormer arranged to have many exotic trees planted around her manor house and several of these can still be seen including a very large Araucaria (or monkey puzzle) tree. The wooded corridors form a natural habitat for birds, including migrant robins from Scandinavia, fungi and, after dusk, bats can often be seen flying in and out of their nesting holes in the sides of the trees.

Bulmer's guide also gave a detailed description of Robin Lythe's Hole:

"The largest and most striking one, Robin Lythe's Hole, is situated under a projection of rock near the North Sea landing-place. The cavern is dimly lighted by two openings - one on the land side, the other looking out on the sea. The former, which is approachable at low water, is the general entrance. For a short distance the passage is low and narrow, then it speedily widens and rises to a height of 60 feet. Approaching the other opening there is a magnificent view outwards, the sea roaring, lashing, foaming, and breaking in spray on the rock beneath. The interior aspect from this spot is truly majestic. The roof is a dome, nearly 50 feet in altitude, formed of arches carved and fretted in a thousand inimitable ways, and here and there in the chalk rock are layers of spar, which the moisture keeps continually wet and shining. The floor has the appearance of a regular flight of stone steps, and, on first entering, should be trodden with care, as the eyes, having been dazzled with the whiteness of the rocks, cannot for some little time penetrate the "tenebrose gloom." This caution is necessary, as the visitor might step into one of the several pools of water scattered over the floor. There is some doubt as to the identity of Robin Lythe, from whom the cavern has obtained its name. According to one tradition he was an honest mariner, who was driven into the cave by the fury of a tempest and providentially saved; but according to another he was a pirate or smuggler, who made use of the cave as a place of concealment for himself and his plunder."

The cave entrance most favoured by visitors is only accessible at low tide and has a shape reminiscent of a sharks tooth. Visitors must check tide times before approaching as the cave does fill with water as the tide comes in. Once inside, the cave opens up to reveal a magnificent, almost cathedral-like chamber lit dimly by the sunshine coming in through the caves second opening. With so many stories of smuggling, shipwrecks and bodies being found in Robin Lythe's Hole it is little wonder that legends exist of a ghostly figure seen rolling a barrel of brandy in the area.

A cautionary tale from the *Shields Daily Gazette* in September 1885 highlighted the risks attached when visiting Robin Lythe's Cave:

"two young gentlemen (one a Wesleyan minister), who were on a visit with some friends at Flamborough, had a very narrow escape from being drowned. They had gone to the North Landing to view Robin Lythe's Cave. They were all cautioned against the attempt, as the sea would reach the cliff at half-flood. They went through the cave, and went on exploring. Suddenly they found to their horror that the rock upon which they were standing was surrounded with water, which was rapidly flowing in. There appeared to them no way of escape. It was in vain they shouted for help. They sprang into the water, and with more good luck than management, another rock was reached. Some of the thoughtful old fishermen had noticed them going into the cave, but had not seen them return. They manned a boat and went in search of them. They were eventually put on shore at the North Landing."

Nowadays the cave attracts specialist cavers and a handful of curious tourists every day, but in Victorian and Edwardian England it was well known and popular with holiday makers along the East Coast. In 1912, a significant rock fall only seemed to add to the interest and intrigue. The *Nottingham Evening Post* reported the incident:

"A remarkable fall of rock, which might have had serious results, had it not occurred during the night, has taken place at Flamborough, a portion of the roof of the noted Smugglers' Cave having collapsed. The cave is visited daily at low tide by hundreds of visitors, who walk over the rocks and climb through a small entrance, where an aged fisherman holds a pair of steps for their convenience. There is a large opening, fifty or sixty yards down, through which the visitor looks out to the open sea, and it is through this opening that the high seas roll when rough weather prevails. On Thursday night a northerly breeze brought very rough seas, and this no

doubt accounts for the fall of the roof which it is thought, may have been originally loosened by the concussion of a heavy artillery gun which used to be fired from the top of the cliff. Inside the cave visitors have had pointed out to them a ledge, which tradition says provided the place where Robin Lythe of smuggling fame, hid when chased by the revenue cutter. It is this ledge which has collapsed."

The *"aged fisherman"* by the way, was John Fell, a lifeboat coxswain from Flamborough, who died at the age of 78 a year after the rock fall.

To see Robin Lythe's Hole without risking life and limb, a visit to nearby Sewerby Hall is advised. There you can view an oil on canvas by J. Walton painted in 1874 that shows the interior of the cave looking back towards the jagged opening and the sea.

Moving a little further to the south, we arrive in Hornsea and find the Strickland family (or more accurately, the Strickland-Constables) once more. Henry Strickland-Constable inherited Wassand Hall in 1874. This is a well-preserved example of a regency house and estate, which almost uniquely has remained in the ownership (and residency) of the same family since it was first built between 1813 and 1819, although the estate of over 1000 acres dates back to 1520.

Bulmer's 1892 Directory gave a guide to St. Nicholas Church in Hornsea accompanied by the following story relating to the vaulted crypt beneath the chancel:

"Many years ago an old woman of weak intellect, known by the soubriquet of Nanny Cankerneedle, took up her abode in it; and it was subjected to still greater profanity by the parish clerk, who used it as a place of concealment for smuggled goods. Whilst engaged in this nefarious occupation, on the night of the 23rd of December, 1782 (the guide differs from other stories where the event occurred some fifty years earlier), *a sudden hurricane arose, which unroofed the church and blew in the great east window. The clerk was stricken with paralysis which deprived him of the power of speech, and the people declared it was a judgment. This violent storm arose from the mere and travelled towards the sea, destroying and unroofing 24 houses (including the Vicarage House), 14 barns, and other outhouses. It overturned the windmill in the*

field called the Dales, and carried the millstones to a distance of 150 yards. Sheets of lead were stript from the church and wrapped round two sycamore trees standing in Hall Garth; and a woman and child, in bed together in one of the unroofed houses, were blown into the street with the bed under them, but fortunately they received no harm."

Legend has it that Cankerneedle was a witch and that a curse was laid upon the parish clerk by her. Apparently, he survived the storm only to die a few months later. One version of the story is that he was so shocked and frightened by the experience that he never spoke again.

The Strickland family had a long association with Flamborough and St. Oswald's Church. The East Window with its seven lights remains as a monument to the late Lady Strickland. Also on display is a replica of Charles II pardon granted to Walter Strickland in 1660. Strickland had been a long-time opponent of Charles I who had him on a charge of high treason after he travelled to Holland to campaign against support being given to the English King.

Remaining in Flamborough, there is the story of young Robin Jewison to tell. The lad was just thirteen years old, when in 1844 he took his pony, Jenny, from his home in Sewerby to the Bending Mule inn at Flamborough in order to replace the pony's shoes. The lad was walking along Croft's Hill approaching the village when he was confronted by a Customs Officer who wanted to know what the boy had seen. *"Nothing untoward"* was his simple response. Robin proceeded to the inn to meet Tanton Pockley, landlord and blacksmith. Inside the Bending Mule the lad could hear sounds coming up from the cellar, but the landlords wife informed him that her husband was bed-ridden by a fever so could not attend to his ponies needs.

Somewhat perturbed by these events and with night closing in, Robin took hold of Jenny and set off for Sewerby. The road was dark and quiet when out of nowhere the shadow of a horse and cart appeared. Robin was looking at the wheels, strangely wrapped in sackcloth and the horses feet similarly covered when a voice remarkably like that of Tanton Pockley spoke to him:

"Now Robin, we've seen a lot of thoo lately and we're allus pleased to meet thoo. But tak our advice. See nowt, hear nowt, and say nowt. One fine day thi grandfather'll mebbe find a bit o' summat extra in' is corn bin. Good neet to thi, Robin."

Jenny tossed her head and took a while for Robin to settle her, by which time the horse, cart and the source of the eerie voice were gone.

The next morning back at Sewerby Robin was greeted by his smiling grandfather – he'd just come across a tub of brandy in his granary!

Some who tell this legend make the most of its spiritual possibilities, but the story is most likely one of smuggling. Tanton Pockley did indeed live for a while at the inn. It had belonged to his father for a time. But Tanton was a draper by trade who went on to be a fishmonger. Birth and census records exist for an R Jewison who lived at Burlington – the old name for Bridlington, of which Sewerby is an outlying village. This lad would have been about the right age for the "legend". We'll obviously never know, but it makes for a good tale – if a tall one.

A woman who undoubtedly also existed was Peg Fyfe. She was definitely from the Market Weighton area and well known up and down the Holderness Coast. Many have told the tale of Peg the witch who skinned people alive, but the truth is that Fyfe was a notorious robber who was not shy of using more than a bit of violence to further her cause. On one occasion, Peg and her band of robbers took a fancy to some horses in Kilnsea. She terrified the farmers young stable lad by telling him to leave the doors to the stables unlocked and not tell a soul or she would remove his skin from his body before his eyes. The frightened stable boy did not know which way to turn so he waited until his master was in the stable and then whispered Peg Fyfe's intentions in the ear of one of the horses – carefully timing his revelation so that the farmer would hear his words too. As a result, when Fyfe and her band turned up that evening, the farmer was waiting for them with his gun loaded. Shots were fired and, although Peg was injured, she and her gang all made their escape – minus their booty of course.

The young stable lad was too frightened to venture out for several weeks, but one day some months later he made the mistake of believing it would now be safe to travel. Peg's band of cronies captured him almost instantly and took him to Peg, who, true to her word, flayed the stable lad mercilessly all over his body including his most sensitive parts, the soles of his feet and the palms of his hands. The legend goes that the boy's cries were so loud and agonising that sailors at sea heard him wailing. When every inch had been flayed Peg let the lad free and he dragged himself back home where he succumbed on his front steps. As for Fyfe, she went on to commit further criminal acts before being captured, tried and hanged for her dastardly deeds.

Peg Fyfe was just one example where the exploits of a common (and brutal) criminal have developed into folk lore legend and become in some ways seen as acceptable, if horrific. Telling tales of witchcraft is more thrilling than narrating stories of crimes and criminals I suppose. Piracy is similar to witchcraft in this respect. What pirates do, and have done for centuries is rob people of possessions and sometimes their lives, ignore laws and use violence indiscriminately. There is nothing romantic or attractive about piracy, as many recent victims off the coast of East Africa will testify. Yet in the eyes of many pirates of old are often given respectability. Perhaps it has something to do with the fact that so many ordinary folk benefitted from their trade in illicit products from gin to tea, gold to flour and so on?

A pirate known well throughout eighteenth century Yorkshire was George Fagg. Like most pirates of the period he had a nickname, but unusually, George had two – so some knew him as *"Snooker"* while others referred to him as *"Stoney"*. His Ship, The *Kent* was a 200 foot schooner built in Folkestone – hence the name – with a 77 foot mainmast, making it fast and manoeuvrable, ideal for carrying heavy loads whilst still being able to outrun and pursuers. With almost two thousand half-ankers of liquor and over 500 oilskin bags of tea on board when The Kent was captured it is easy to see how much wealthy those who made a living from piracy could become. Just one half-anker tub of gin can fill over 30 bottles, remember. The ship alone was valued at well over a thousand pounds. Tea was a popular import – it was lightweight and carried an enormous mark-up. In the second half of the eighteenth century, tea could be bought throughout Europe for as little as seven pence per pound and then sold on in England for as much as 5 shillings a pound – a profit of over 800%!

Gin and brandy would usually be watered down before bottling to secure a similar profit margin. Fagg, like other smugglers, had no shortage of customers and people willing to help conceal his contraband. Unlike now when most illegal imports are fake goods, often containing dangerous levels of toxins, in Fagg's time, smugglers like him were bringing in the real stuff, just avoiding paying any duties to the Crown.

Large sums of money were spent trying to put a stop to smuggling. Ships were constantly scouring the coastline in search of pirates, while customs men visited coastal settlements in search of information from whistle-blowers. It has to be said that efforts to stop and catch the likes of Fagg were sometimes half-baked at best. Captain Mitchell of the *Swallow*, a small Revenue Cutter encountered Fagg on several occasions in the Spring and early summer of 1777, but avoided confronting him on each instance. There were even stories of Fagg inviting revenue men on board the *Kent* whilst moored at Bridlington and offering them gin and supplies when he heard that they were short-stocked themselves.

Eventually, though, Fagg's days were numbered. In July 1777, Scottish Revenue Officers got news that Fagg was on board the *Kent*, moored off Flamborough Head. Dissatisfied with the failed efforts of Captain Mitchell, they resolved to dispatch two of their own vessels to deal with Fagg once and for all. The *Royal George* and the *Prince of Wales* ran south from St. Abb's Head in Berwickshire and met up with the *Kent* in Filey Bay. With the unintended support of two naval vessels, HMS *Arethusa* and *Pelican,* the *Kent's* armoury of swivel guns, cannon, blunderbusses and muskets was no match. After a fierce defence lasting several hours, The *Kent* was boarded and Fagg along with his crew of 39 men were taken into custody. Many of the men were taken from rowing boats which had been lashed to Fagg's crippled ship in a final desperate effort to escape. With several thousand pounds worth of contraband and a bounty of £100 to collect it was a good day for the revenue men. Five crewman on the *Kent* lost their lives in the afternoon's battles. News spread rapidly, but it was not popular with residents of seaside towns such as Scarborough where the smugglers were seen as a source of cheap goods and the revenue men were widely regarded as the bad guys.

What became of George Fagg is unclear. A smuggler by the same name, commanding the *Rose* along the south coast of England was captured after a long and bloody battle in 1781 – whether this is the same man is the subject of some speculation. So we end where we began – some popular legends are indeed based on fact, some are unverified, while others are no more than the stuff of myth.

Further Reading

Curious Tales of Old East Yorkshire, Howard Peach, Sigma Press (2001)

The Fine Art of Smuggling, E Keble Chatterton, Fireship Press (2008)

N is for National Trail – The coastal part of the Cleveland Way

England has twelve National Trails, two of which can be walked in Yorkshire. The Yorkshire Wolds Way connects Filey with Hessle on the outskirts of Hull and is a beautiful walk of some 80 miles, but as this is a book about the Yorkshire Coast, I will leave this for another time. However, a National Trail that covers the entire coastline between Saltburn and Filey is very deserving of closer scrutiny.

Map 25: Filey – Scarborough Section

https://www.google.com/maps/d/edit?mid=zR-wiCMof9PQ.kqPC0m7WREDc&usp=sharing

Map 26: Scarborough – Whitby Section

https://www.google.com/maps/d/edit?mid=zR-wiCMof9PQ.kZnnB11ZF37A&usp=sharing

Map 27: Whitby – Saltburn Section

https://www.google.com/maps/d/edit?mid=zR-wiCMof9PQ.kyavBZFtZIDo&usp=sharing

The Cleveland Way is roughly horseshoe-shaped joining Helmsley on the edge of the North Yorks Moors National Park with Filey (or more accurately Carr Naze above Filey Brigg). The concept of a long-distance footpath linking several independent coastal paths before wending its way through inland northern Yorkshire was first proposed in the 1930's by the Teesside Ramblers Association. It took 20 years to submit detailed plans for consideration and a further 15 years until the official opening of the complete trail. Since nearly half of the Cleveland Way's 110 miles follows the coastline between Filey and Saltburn it is this that we shall consider.

There is something very satisfying about following in the footsteps of previous generations of visitors to the Yorkshire Coast. The Cleveland Way has more than its fair share of famous passers-through from the past. For example, just to the south of Scarborough the path follows the line of Black Rocks – one of several scenes sketched or painted by JMW Turner in the early part of the nineteenth century. Beast Cliff at Staitondale may not have any household names in its ancestry but as an area of Special Scientific Interest, this part of the footpath attracts botanists and fossil-hunters as well as many keen to see the range of barrows and tumuli that point at settlements existing here several thousand years ago. Further north at Brackenberry Wyke, which like Beast Cliff is surely worth visiting just for its name, a diversion of just a few yards from the footpath is all it takes to see the remains of old ironstone works and fossilised remains dating back millions of years.

How you choose to follow a National Trail is up to you. I've split the coastal path into three sections as much for the convenience of viewing the landmarks on maps as anything else. There will be some who would walk the whole coastline in a weekend, while others may stroll a little bit here, another there and take several visits to complete the fifty miles of footpaths, roadsides and in some cases, sandy beaches. Be aware that my three sections are not equal in length. The path between Filey and Scarborough at only 9 miles is easily the shortest "third", while the middle section between Whitby and Scarborough is the longest at around 22 miles.

Many of the towns and villages along the trail are reasonably well served by public transport, so one possibility is to base yourself in the larger towns such as Saltburn, Scarborough or Whitby, do as much walking as you feel able each day and then get the bus back to base (or vice versa). This is particularly useful if you are unable to carry your luggage with you every day.

Please remember that this is a very dynamic coastline – to look at and in its form. The Cleveland Way does change regularly as sections are lost to coastal erosion so check online before visiting and take notice of any information warning you of hazards. If it looks risky, or the advice is to avoid – then find a safer path. Also, this is a popular trail but some sections are very quiet – you may not meet many other people and you are likely to be out of range of mobile phone signals at times.

I've chosen to describe the route from South to North, but of course, you can go whichever way you prefer. My preference is to have the prevailing wind behind me, but when there is a cool northerly blowing, it may well feel less chilly to walk towards the South.

The Cleveland Way, as with all National Trails uses the "acorn symbol" to waymark the entire length at key points. In times gone by, there would have been no signposts, just a worn path along a clifftop to follow. There is something hugely satisfying about following in the footsteps of human beings going back perhaps thousands of years.

Since this is not a circular walk you will inevitably finish each day in a different location to the place where you started so accommodation planning can be a little awkward. My advice is to take a look online at services that offer to help with your planning even to the point of picking up your baggage each morning and delivering it to your next stopover – for a small fee, of course.

Should you find that any part of the Cleveland Way is blocked, closed or unavailable for any reason, please find a safe (and legal) alternative route. Remember that a flat wide beach may look inviting for a walk, but when the tide is in do you have a safe exit? Fences and walls aren't just boundary markers, they are there often there to keep livestock in and trespassers out. I find it is always advisable to check the availability of routes online before setting off on a walk.

A final thought. Why not customise your walking route to take in some of the other shorter but equally fascinating and rewarding trails in the locality. For example, the old Scarborough to Whitby Railway line is now a trail of almost 20 miles in length, suitable for walkers or cyclists that includes the spectacular viaduct over the River Esk on the fringes of Whitby. Also, at Ravenscar a circular trail – the Ravenscar Round – offers an interesting 6-mile diversion with stunning views.

Further Reading

The Cleveland Way and The Yorkshire Wolds Way, Paddy Dillon, Cicerone Press (2010)

The Cleveland Way, Ian Sampson, Aurum Press (2012)

O is for Orca – Whale Spotting on the Yorkshire Coast

Cetaceans are marine mammals that share common features. They are all known to be highly intelligent and are relatively easy to spot compared to many species of fish as they all have blowholes and need to surface periodically in order to breathe.

Map 28: Locations where you can take to the seas in search of porpoises, dolphins and whales.

https://www.google.com/maps/d/edit?mid=zR-wiCMof9PQ.kkSHzojjxQBM&usp=sharing

Of course, if you go out to sea in search of a whale, there is no guarantee you will actually see one, but local advice is that the later summer and early autumn are possibly your best times to look. From July onwards, Whales can often be found tracking mackerel and herring along the coastline.

If you don't get to see a whale, you have a much better chance of spotting one of several types of porpoise or dolphin that frequent these waters. Harbour porpoises were given their name for an obvious reason – they prefer shallow waters particularly around estuaries, fjords and … harbours. They have been known to follow rivers upstream, often travelling miles from the ocean. Harbour porpoises are often mistaken for small, or young dolphins, and whilst there are similarities, they do tend to keep apart. In fact, researchers have discovered that bottlenose dolphins will sometimes attack and kill their smaller cousins to prevent them from competing with them for food. Grey seals, which can also be seen in these parts, have also been seen attacking harbour porpoises, presumably as they are a very good source of fat.

So, how do you tell a harbour porpoise from a dolphin? Firstly, size – the harbour porpoise is one of the smallest marine mammals, and rarely grows longer than 6 feet, even in full maturity. If you get close enough, dolphins have long beak jaws whereas porpoises lack a beak, having a blunt jaw and a much smaller head. Perhaps the most visible sign when viewing from a distance is the distinctive dorsal fin of the harbour porpoise. It is much smaller than that of a dolphin and very obviously triangular in shape. Finally, it is behaviour that will help you to tell the difference. Dolphins are much more social and will most likely be spotted in pods – often several dozen at a time – whereas the harbour porpoise is a more solitary marine mammal.

The minke whale is being seen in increasing numbers up and down the Yorkshire coast. It too has a distinctive dorsal fin. It is proportionately smaller than that of other species of whales and is also noticeably curved. If you are in a boat and get close enough, the way to tell a minke whale from other whales is to look for white bands on each of its flippers. As whales go, the minke is one of the smaller ones – but if you see a fully grown adult female at 8 metres long and weighing in at around 4 and a half tons, you probably wouldn't use the word small in your description! One thing to look out for if you see a minke whale is an arching of its back. This is the last thing it usually does before diving. But don't expect a chance to set up that most iconic of shots of the tail fluke. Unlike the larger Humpback, the minke does not lift its fluke out of the water when it dives. Research by the Sea Watch Foundation suggests there may be as many as 100,000 minke whales in the North Sea and that the best time to see them close to land is in the late summer.

Killer Whales are less frequent visitors to the Yorkshire coast, but you might just spot one if you are lucky. In times past the name grampus was given to Orcas, although species identification was not always reliable, so the name was often applied to other whales and even larger dolphins. Sadly, most people's only sighting of a whale was when one washed ashore. In addition, it has seemed that throughout history the only newsworthy sighting of a whale was if it was a dead or dying one. The *Newcastle Courant* carried the following report of such an instance in October 1789:

"a grampus came ashore in Filey Bay, which some fishermen killed with a hay-spade. It measured 32 feet in length and 16 in circumference. Many

people from Scarbrough (sic) and other places visited Filey, in order to view so rare a curiosity."

Fortuitously someone thought to measure the poor animal, whose size does in fact suggest it may well have been a lost, ill or injured killer whale. The death of a stranded whale is an emotional experience for all involved and thankfully it doesn't happen all that often. In March 1910 at Cloughton Wyke a 51-foot-long Lesser Rorqual whale was stranded on rocks in an unrecoverable position. Six months later the carcass of another whale 20 feet longer washed up at the same location.

In January 1937 at Bridlington the death of a male sperm whale provided a local fellmonger with a somewhat unusual business opportunity as the *Yorkshire Evening Post* revealed to its readers. Apparently, Bridlington Corporation struck a deal with a local fellmonger by the name of F. Coates whereby the whale became the property of Coates provided that he promptly removed it from the beach. The newspaper reported Coates to be *"satisfied with the results of the bargain"*. After removing in excess of 50 tons of flesh from the skeleton and skull (which some newspapers reported that he sold to the Natural History Museum in London), Coates had ended up with a yield of *"about 400 gallons"* of oil. With a retail value of around £20 a barrel, Coates had every reason to be pleased with his work. It would appear unlikely that the four tons of bones would have contributed to Coates' financial haul since a *"fishes royal"* statute dating back as far as the reign of Edward II makes every whale landed on the coast of England and Wales the property of the reigning monarch.

What causes whales to become stranded is a matter of some debate. In fact, there are several possible reasons. Many, if not most, whales are washed up having already died from natural causes at sea. Sometimes, particularly where coastlines are very shallow, whales have been known to follow dolphins and porpoises who manage with significantly less water. Rough seas, getting lost, even following food such as squid can all lead to beaching with tragic consequences. One final possibility is that the whale was driven out of its herd by other stronger bull whales. This particular male may or may not have been alive when washed up on that cold January day in 1937. The *Hull Daily Mail* reported that fishermen who had first sighted *"one of the biggest monsters of the sea"* at about 5.30

a.m. deduced it still to be living because *"as one man attempted to pierce the flesh the monster spurted out a jet of blood"*. There are probably much better ways to look for vital life signs in a beached whale.

The Spurn Peninsula and Humber Estuary has a well-documented history of multiple cetacean visits. Nowadays, whale spotters are generally satisfied with a sighting and perhaps a few photographs or video clips as souvenirs. This has not always been the case as the *Sheffield Independent* reported in 1879. Apparently two men walking along the shoreline saw a *"large number of huge fish floundering"*. Closer observation revealed that three whales had been shot and were already dead or near death. The men sought the assistance of a couple of ballast lighters onboard a nearby boat who slaughtered the other four with a knife and crowbar. The *Leeds Mercury* had already identified the killers of the first three whales as two local clergymen, who retained one of the carcasses as a *"trophy"*. The remaining six, probably all young whales were taken to Hull and then on to Leeds and Sheffield to be exhibition pieces.

Mercifully these days the human tendency is to photograph or video evidence of marine wildlife and exhibit such virtual trophies online for all to see, without harming any of the wonderful creatures of the seas. The Yorkshire Wildlife Trust and Royal Society for the Protection of Birds regularly update their websites when important sightings are made.

Seals are most likely going to be the easiest marine mammals to see, often up close and personal – so long as you know where to look and how to treat them with respect. Perhaps the best place to go is *the village that never was* – Ravenscar, where large colonies of grey and common seals coexist happily. Common seals give birth to pups during June or July, while the greys pup later in November. Look out for them on rocks or even on the beach when the tide is out. Remember these marine mammals are easily shocked so keep your distance and do not allow dogs to approach them. Grey Seal pups, which are actually white, tend to stay ashore until their coats have moulted and they have gained substantial amounts of weight. The Spurn Peninsula in early winter is often a good place to spot these very photogenic but frequently persecuted mammals.

Most of your viewing will not be on land however and the sea is a vast thing, so where do you look – you can't have your eyes everywhere. There are clues on the water and in the air. Look out for those silvery tracks on the surface of the water. They are always there and whales in particular use them to help them follow the coastline. Also, look out for the behaviour of the flocks of seabirds. Anywhere that you can see large flocks of birds feeding on fish is also a possible location for whales. If the birds suddenly appear startled, it may well be the presence of a whale that has caused them to fly.

The North Sea is a surprisingly biodiverse place considering that it is one of the world's smaller expanses of salt water. Pinnipeds (that's seals to most of us) come in a variety of shapes and sizes. Although generally seen further north, bearded, ringed, hooded and harp seals have all been known to explore the waters of the Yorkshire coast from time to time. Sadly, human intervention has led to the decline of many species, once common in our waters. Sturgeon, skates and salmon were all fished to the point of elimination. Believe it or not, pelicans and flamingoes were once commonplace too.

The outlook for marine wildlife and mammals in particular is not promising. In spite of concerted efforts by marine conservation organisations as well as national and international legislation the North Sea continues to be a major worry for scientists and economists. Climate change, the legacy of over-fishing, the introduction of non-indigenous species, pollution, increasing marine traffic and off-shore industrialisation combine to create a most problematic whirlpool that cannot be stopped with a single solution. Part of the problem is that most of us just don't see it happening. Problems on land are often under our noses – what is going on out at sea may well have even more disastrous consequences.

Further Reading

Yorkshire's Whales, Dolphins and Porpoises, Robin Petch & Kris Simpson, Blurb (2015)

P is for Piers, Pierrots and Promenades

The transformation of seaside communities from settlements where fishing and farming dominate to holiday towns, mostly reliant on income from tourism was initially fast, furious and very rewarding but as times, and particularly fashions have changed, many of these towns and villages are now having to rethink their priorities and re-invent themselves once more.

Map 29: Bridlington old and new

https://www.google.com/maps/d/edit?mid=zR-wiCMof9PQ.kwuGSik2vuTo&usp=sharing

Map 30: A short historical guide to Hornsea

https://www.google.com/maps/d/edit?mid=zR-wiCMof9PQ.kpOM1CT45GNQ&usp=sharing

Map 31: A walk along the seafront between Saltburn and Marske

https://www.google.com/maps/d/edit?mid=zR-wiCMof9PQ.ksy2tPKFDeQQ&usp=sharing

Take Bridlington, for example. In the early part of the nineteenth century the harbour was thriving. Over 100 grain ships came and went in a typical year. Every week a service ran between here and London, tea was imported into Bridlington from Europe and fishing boats ran in and out of the harbour on a daily basis. There was work for most who lived here, either on the boats, building and maintaining them or working with their produce. The harbour area received major investment between 1816 and 1835 to build the two long stone piers that we see today, but the steam engine was to give the port a double jolt.

Firstly, the ships themselves became bigger and faster as they increasingly became steam powered. Bridlington was neither equipped to build steamers or capable of handling them in its relatively small and tight harbour. Secondly, the rapid rise of the steam railways in England meant that goods which traditionally moved by sea could be transported around the country much more efficiently by rail. It is no coincidence that Bridlington got a railway station in 1846, three years after the last Bridlington boat was built and that by the 1860s only a handful of boats were using the harbour regularly.

As with many other coastal locations the railway enabled Bridlington to expand as a venue for holidaymakers. In 1811 Benjamin Milne, the towns customs collector, discovered a spring flowing into the harbour and, seeing the potential benefits, a three inch copper pipe was sunk through the clay to "tap" the water supply. Analysis a few years later revealed the water to be about as pure as it could get. In fact, William White described it as *"so pure and soft, that it is used in the washing of the finest linen, and so copious, that it would supply the whole navy of England"*. A chalybeate spring had also been discovered to the north-west of the quay and visitors flocked to "benefit" *from these "health-giving"* waters. The Spa complex actually came much later. The Whitaker Brothers of Leeds were contracted to build the sea wall and New Spa and Gardens, which opened to the public in 1896. The five acre site included a theatre, concert hall, glass-covered bandstand and landscaped gardens around a pool fed from the nearby spring. Crowds flocked day and night (it was one of the first seaside places to feature electrical illuminations), paying just a few pennies each to pass through a turnstile to enter the new attraction. As many as 80,000 visitors were recorded in a single month.

The Spa has a checkered history, twice fire has raged through its buildings and twice it has re-invented itself. The latest refurbishments, completed in 2008 have brought the complex up to date as a concert venue, Conference Centre, theatre and café bar. These days it is a popular with families during the day and draws in a wide range of audiences for its evening attractions.

In early Victorian times the most popular forms of entertainment were those that did not require any expense. Strolling along the seafront was deemed to be good for the health and soul – and it did not cost any money. Bathing in the sea was also free, but in those days of modesty, bathers often wore as much if not more than they would wear on dry land. Entrepreneurs were quick to realise that money was to be made from renting out beach huts or chalets in which revelers could change attire without fear of embarrassment. Bathing machines encouraged even more modesty. Think of a garden shed with a door at both ends and put it on wheels and you're about there. These were generally designed with ladies in mind. Entry would be made, fully clothed, on the beach. Upon the occupants signal the bathing machine would be pulled – usually by a horse, pony or donkey - into the sea thereby enabling the bather to emerge directly into the water without being seen in a state of inappropriate undress! James Meggison was one such entrepreneur. His 1841 census entry describes him simply as *"bathing man"* when he actually was co-owner of a business operating dozens of bathing machines running up and down the beach all day during the summer season. Bathing machines were incredibly popular, but were also a source of much stress and aggravation. A flat fee was paid for the hire of a machine, regardless of the amount of time taken to change inside one. Queues often formed and arguments between prospective customers and owners were a frequent site.

As time went on and the concept of taking a seaside holiday as a break from routine rather than to cure some ailment or other took off, entrepreneurs found more and more ways for visitors to part with their money. Up the coast in Saltburn, the Pease family spent much of the second half of the nineteenth century building a cliff top seaside town but it was John Anderson, a railway engineer who was largely responsible for developing "new" Saltburn as a holiday resort. Anderson had engineered the railway line and station connecting Saltburn with Stockton, Darlington, York and Newcastle. Six years after the station opened in 1861, Anderson formed the Saltburn Pier Company. He was a much-travelled man who was always capable of taking one idea and transferring it elsewhere. In Margate was a pier with no rivals – this would be the basis for John's Saltburn Pier.

It took over a year and a half to construct, but when it opened in the summer of 1869 it was a magnificent sight and an instant success. By the end of the year more than 50,000 visitors had paid to gain entry. The only thing that pier-goers didn't like was the long and arduous walk down to the pier from the new town at the top of the cliff, followed by the even more strenuous trip back up later. Anderson's solution to this, which opened the following year was a wooden cliff hoist. This involved walking along an elevated wooden footpath to a large cage counterbalanced with a water container. The cage allowed up to twenty people at a time to travel to and from the pier 120 feet below. It was a precarious structure and after thirteen years the wooden hoist was condemned as unsafe. Enter one George Marks who designed and oversaw the construction of a funicular railway system similar to those already operating in Scarborough. This opened in 1884 and, other than basic maintenance and cosmetic alterations, little has changed since.

The pier meantime drew large crowds year on year. From 1870, boat trips to and from Hartlepool and Middlesbrough ran regularly off the pier ends landing stage. Until 1875 everything went very well indeed. On the night of Thursday 14th October the North East coast was battered by storm force winds. The following morning residents of Saltburn awoke to find the final 300 feet of their precious pier had been quite literally blown away. A reporter for the *Middlesbrough Daily Gazette* observed that *"elm planks, thirteen inches square, were snapped like matches, and spread along the beach as far as Redcar Pier."* Somewhat unwisely, the owners chose not to replace the lost section and the pier continued to operate minus its landing stage and boat trips. As a result visitor numbers declined and the future of the pier was in doubt. The opening of the funicular railway revitalised public interest in the pier eight years later and substantial amounts of money were invested in the erection of a saloon bar, bandstand and refreshment rooms. Gas lighting was installed along the full length of the pier (replaced by electric lights – a somewhat safer choice on a wooden pier – three years later) allowing it to shine brightly throughout the night. Since then the pier has been struck by a ship, damaged by storms, even partly dismantled during World War II to prevent the Germans from using it to invade England, but it remains to this day a popular landmark. It is now a Grade II Listed Building and in 2009 was awarded the title of pier of the year.

Bridlington has the distinction of affording holidaymakers not one but two promenades either side of the towns central harbour. In fact, since a recent extensive remodelling programme, the south promenade is actually three connected promenades offering a walk of over a mile in length with several themed art works and installations celebrating the town's history and relationship with the North Sea. In spite of this revitalisation, it is still dwarfed by the similarly updated North Promenade (again strictly speaking, not one, since it was first constructed as several terraced promenades) stretching out over two miles giving visitors the opportunity to walk or even cycle all the way to Sewerby Hall and back.

Sea Walls and promenades generally go hand in hand. To construct a sea wall capable of withstanding the worst that nature can almost literally throw at it requires an immense engineering project and inevitably leads to significant changes to both the shoreline and the land immediately behind it. The design of the seawall itself can sometimes be used to enhance the seaward side, for example by using steps to dissipate wave energy. This simultaneously provides level, often dry, areas for visitors to sit and admire the view without getting too much sand between the toes. A good example is Scarborough North Bay. Curved sea walls such as that at Filey are designed to throw wave energy back at the sea, both diverting power and using it to "break" further incoming waves. The simplest (and usually cheapest) to construct are vertical sea walls like the very tall one at Robin Hood's Bay. These can be quite effective but are also prone to damage requiring repeated and extensive repairs over time. Whatever type of sea wall is engineered, the obvious architectural solution to issue of how to leave the landward side is to construct a promenade.

Saltburn-by-the-Sea took shape during the latter stages of the nineteenth century at a time when promenading was an essential part of any seaside visit. The only trouble was that the "new" Saltburn stood on the top of a cliff. The solution – two promenades. A lower one at seafront level and a second along the clifftop.

A promenade can also conceal essential features that might otherwise detract from the seaside ambience. Take Filey, for example. I doubt that many who stroll along its lovely promenade realise that in the central section they are walking on top of a multi-million-pound water pumping station processing much of the areas treated sewage and simultaneously ensuring that Filey Bay has some of the cleanest bathing water in Europe.

If holidaymakers were not happy promenading alongside the sea or strolling above it up and down a wooden pier, then there were always the Pierrots to entertain them. The Holderness coastal town of Hornsea had a short-lived pier. Opened in 1880, like its bigger brother at Saltburn it was struck by a boat, the *Earl of Derby* just a few months later and never recovered, finally being demolished in 1897. Four crew members of the Earl of Derby were feared to have drowned in the collision until, as the *York Herald* reported the following day that the men had *"clambered on to the pier and walked to the station."* The promenade at Hornsea has fared much better. The beach at Hornsea is long, wide and very straight and the promenade has always been a popular place to stroll. In 2003 an extensive renewal of its central promenade saw it brought right up to date with a series of gardens, placed to coincide with the groynes running out to sea. A hundred years ago gardens would have been a welcome sight for the eyes, but the fashionable entertainment in those days was provided by bands of Pierrots.

The first Pierrot troupes appeared in England from 1891 but soon became common sights on seafronts up and down the land. Clifford Essex is widely credited as having introduced Pierrot shows to the Henley Regatta and later in 1891 at Cowes on the Isle of Wight, having seen a performance of *L'Enfant Prodigue* at The Prince of Wales Theatre in London. The show featured a family of Pierrots and Essex left inspired to dress his musicians in white satin, pompoms and ruffles. His Pierrots were seen by thousands and copied hundreds of times over.

At Hornsea, like many other locations without a permanent venue, the Pierrots provided their entertainment shows from temporary stages erected on the beach facing the promenade. Large crowds were attracted to watch, but in an open space it was difficult to manage ticket sales and many got a free show. In 1913, with money originally set aside to replace the ill-fated pier, a large cast-iron and glass pavilion was opened on the seafront. The Floral Hall went on to become the home of the Pierrots for many years.

Pierrots attracted interest from all over the country and any addition to a local troupe was reported widely. Nowadays a man walking along a seafront promenade on stilts may not even turn the eye for many, but in

1899 news of *"a pierrot mounted on lofty stilts"* at Hornsea made it onto the pages of the *Hull Daily Mail* newspaper. Between 1900 and 1930 at least five different Pierrot troupes performed at Hornsea alone. Working as a Pierrot meant long hours and often with little financial reward. Often performing in the open-air, Pierrot troupes were reliant on both the weather and the honesty of their audiences. In many locations, payment was made by *"bottling"* – a glass bottle would have a slot cut in the side for coins to be deposited and at the end of the show the bottles would be smashed and the takings shared. Bank holidays were potentially bonanza paydays. In 1871 the Bank Holiday Act gave every worker four paid days leave annually – Boxing Day, Easter Monday, Whit Monday plus the first Monday in August. For three of those days Pierrots would be waiting at the railway station and walking along the promenade from early morning drumming up interest in their three performances – one later in the morning and two afternoon shows. Incomes were supplemented by hiring out deckchairs and selling postcards.

An influx of army recruits training at Hornsea helped to maintain interest in the Pierrots during the years of World War I. Some soldiers even banded together to form their own temporary troupes before being sent off to fight. Pierrot troupes often gave future stars their performing break. Stanley Holloway, Arthur Askey and Leslie Crowther all started their careers at the seaside in this way.

Will Catlin ran a very successful touring Pierrot show for over two decades, appearing regularly at Hornsea, Bridlington, Filey and Scarborough. A blue plaque on the site of the former Arcadia Theatre in Scarborough commemorates his troupes shows there between 1909 and 1921. He was a shrewd businessman as well as being a born entertainer. Catlin had been born William Fox in Leicestershire but changed his surname so that it sounded better when said alongside his music hall partner Charlie Carson. When he started his pierrot show he soon spotted that his audience included large numbers of young ladies so he refused to employ any female performers and insisted that all members of his troupe gave the appearance of being eligible bachelors at all times – even if they were married. Catlin also realised that earnings from the summer season alone would not provide enough for his performers to manage all year round, so he hired concert halls in inland towns and cities and put on pierrot shows throughout the colder months as well as seaside summer performances.

Further Reading

Pierrots of the Yorkshire Coast, Chapman Mave & Ben, Hutton Press (1988)

Q is for Queen of the Yorkshire Coast

Scarborough has often been labelled "Queen of the Yorkshire Coast". Indeed, tourist brochures and websites still frequently like to use the tag in their promotional literature. Paul Allen in his biography of local playwright Alan Ayckbourn claimed that many Scarborians held the view that in the years immediately after the Second World War the town was no longer worthy of the accolade. Scarborough has changed, and continues to do so as does the Royal Family. Regardless of Scarborough's entitlement to Monarch status, just how has it been connected with the monarchy over the centuries?

Map 32: Scarborough landmarks associated with royalty

https://www.google.com/maps/d/edit?mid=zR-wiCMof9PQ.kEcoOfYcBQ1k&usp=sharing

Let's start with Queen Victoria. Scarborough is by no means unique in having a road and a street named after her. There are more than sixty statues of Queen Victoria throughout England so it is no surprise that Scarborough has one too. This one was positioned outside the newly-built town hall in 1903 and was unveiled by her daughter Beatrice, Princess Henry of Battenburg. Close examination of the bronze statue reveals Victoria to be wearing a Star of India on her breast. This was probably included by the statue's designer Charles Bell Birch who was commissioned to produce a statue to mark the Queen's Golden Jubilee. The original, 4-metre-high Carrara marble statue, of which the one in Scarborough is a copy, was sent to Udaipur in India, where it remained until independence in 1947. At least seven other bronze copies were made. One of them is in Victoria Square, Adelaide, Australia. Queen Victoria never actually visited Scarborough.

Another of Victoria and Albert's offspring to visit Scarborough was their seventh child, Prince Arthur, the Duke of Connaught who came to the town in August 1908 with his wife Princess Louise Margaret of Prussia, the Duchess of Connaught. The occasion was the opening of Marine Drive. Speaking of his pride at being asked to open the *"magnificent parade"* the Duke acknowledged the *"time, money and anxiety"* involved in the completion of this mammoth engineering project. Arthur also referred to the loss of his oldest brother in 1892 from influenza.

Marine Drive was envisaged as serving two key purposes. Firstly, it would create a much needed defensive sea wall. The headland on which Scarborough Castle sat was eroding at such a rate that engineers estimated the castle itself would be lost to the sea in less than a hundred years. Secondly, expensive promenades had been completed along both North Bay and South Bay, but for most visitors wanting to stroll between the two bays meant a long, meandering walk up and down very steep paths – Marine drive would wind around the headland, connecting both promenades at a stroke. It was to be a long stroke. Foundations were laid in 1897 with the project scheduled to take three years and cost a little under £70,000. Three years passed with little to show for it. Bad weather and poor management took an equal share of the blame. It took seven years to complete construction, but storms immediately washed away the North Pier and caused considerable damage to the new sea wall. Repairs were not completed until the end of 1907 but a further storm during January 1908 led to a large section of the wall moving seaward leaving a 400-foot section of the newly surfaced drive with deep, foot wide cracks. After additional extensive repairs, the public first made use of the new Marine Drive in April 1908, four months before the opening ceremony, but eight years late. The final cost was nearly £125,000 – almost double the original estimate.

Some might think that Royal Albert Park and Royal Albert Drive were named in honour of Queen Victoria's late husband Prince Albert. Work on Royal Albert Drive was completed in 1890, some 18 years prior to Marine Drive. The Duke of Clarence and Avondale, Prince Albert, the eldest son of Albert Edward, and, therefore, Grandson of Victoria, accepted an invitation to visit Scarborough for the opening ceremony of what was originally known as the North Parade. This sea wall and promenade had been started in 1887 and was effectively a scaled-back version of the later project to build Marine Drive. At the time, council funding would not stretch to the more ambitious project so an area stretching 1200 yards from Castle Holms (Now Royal Albert Park) to Peasholme Beck was prioritised. This earlier project also came in significantly over budget, costing almost 50% more than the original £30,000 estimate, but at least it managed to be completed in three years.

The Duke of Clarence's father Albert Edward (who became Edward VII) stayed in Scarborough in the Autumn of 1871. Suitable accommodation for the Prince of Wales, his wife and young family was found on the stylish Crescent at Londesborough Lodge. Before leaving for Sandringham, a letter was dispatched to the Mayor of Scarborough indicating clearly that *"The Prince and Princess of Wales cannot leave Scarborough without [expressing] to the inhabitants how much gratified they have been with the magnificent reception they have met with"*. A few days later Bertie as he was known fell ill. Doctors at Sandringham diagnosed Typhoid fever. Ten years earlier his father had died, almost certainly from the same disease. Victoria visited her son on December 14th – the anniversary of her husband's death. Miraculously he began to recover. Londesborough Lodge was the subject of intense scrutiny and speculation, as was every other royal household, including Buckingham Palace. No firm conclusion could be reached about Londesborough Lodge, in spite of the deaths of two others residing there at the same time as the Prince of Wales. The Lancet published the results of an investigation with claims of an open cesspool directly beneath the Prince's latrine. However, several newspapers subsequently published independent engineering reports showing this not to be the case at all. The only conclusive evidence came from Buckingham Palace where all bar one of the sanitary devices was found to be defective – and that one was exclusively used by servants.

More recently, on October 23rd 1936, Prince George, the Duke of Kent visited Scarborough to open the town's new Hospital Buildings. Some of the £135,000 needed to construct the new hospital came from the sale of the Cottage Hospital on Springhill Road. This hospital had been founded by the widow of a surgeon from Birmingham 65 years earlier and had served the medical needs of many Scarborians until it was forced to close during the economic recession of 1931. The Ann Wright Ward at Scarborough General Hospital is named in her honour.

Until 1975, the most recent visit to Scarborough by a reigning monarch had been that of Richard III in 1484. Queen Elizabeth II has been to Scarborough twice. Her first visit on 2nd July 1975 saw her arrive at Scarborough Railway Station shortly after 10 a.m. accompanied by her husband, the Duke of Edinburgh. Crowds lined the route as a limousine drove the Queen and Prince Phillip down Columbus Ravine before arriving at Scalby Lodge Farm, part of a large estate in the ownership of the Duchy of Lancaster. As always with any Royal visit, timekeeping had to be meticulous. A large marquee had been erected so that invited guests could receive the royal party, who arrived bang on time at 10.25 a.m. They stayed for exactly 35 minutes before travelling on to visit a tenant in Cloughton, a farm in Brompton and the nearby town of Pickering. In 2010 the Queen visited Scarborough for a second time, primarily to see the revamped open-air theatre. On this occasion the royal party, numbering some 60 people in total, stopped off at the Blacksmiths Arms in Cloughton for a lunch engagement.

King George IV never made it to Scarborough, but he did sail past – twice. Whilst the King travelled north in early August 1822 a deputation of officials from Scarborough including the Mayor in his robes set sail aboard the schooner Moscow to greet him. The speed of the King George was too much for the schooner and so the deputation was unable to hold steady alongside for long enough to board the Royal yacht. This led to a situation observed *"with some little merriment"* by the sailors (Saunders Newsletter, 19th August 1822) where the Mayor was forced to pass his welcoming address to the King's representative on the end of a long pole. A royal salute was also fired by cannon from Scarborough itself. Many local people as well as holidaymakers put to sea in a variety of crafts hoping to catch a glimpse of the King. Later in the month on his return journey from Scotland, the King George sailed past Scarborough again. This time a cannon salute was again fired but the Mayor and corporation members chose to stay ashore.

When royalty come to town, people will often go to extraordinary lengths to get a view. For the visit of Princess Henry of Battenberg on 28th July 1903, thousands lined the streets. The Princess spent just over three hours in Scarborough, but, as the *Sheffield Daily Telegraph* reported the following morning, she had a hectic schedule *"her Royal Highness* inspected the hospital, received gifts for the institution, opened the new Town Hall, unveiled a Roll of Honour, received an address of welcome, held a reception, unveiled a statue of her beloved mother, and attended a public luncheon." The week had begun with a very wet Monday. For the royal visit the following day, skies remained overcast and a stiff breeze blew throughout the streets. As the newspaper stated "The town was gaily decorated (with) an abundance of flags and paper flowers everywhere." The "Roll of Honour" referred to in the article is a dedication to the fifty volunteer men of Scarborough who served in the South African (or Boer) War between 1899 and 1902. This can still be viewed inside the Town Hall.

You might be wondering where the Princess stayed? Scarborough had several suitable options, but the Princess had a close acquaintance nearby. Lord Cecil, formerly secretary to the Princess's late husband was occupying Hunmanby Hall near Filey. Princess Henry chose to stay with her friend. A large Copper Beech tree in front of the hall was planted by the princess during her stay.

King Richard III visited Scarborough several times during 1484. There is no doubt about his first visit during May, or second visit in early July. Documents sealed by the King between May 22nd and July 5th were clearly marked as originating from the castle. Later sealed orders only indicated Scarborough as the origin, leading to many to speculate that the King sought alternative accommodation. Richard was in Scarborough to assemble and ready a fleet in anticipation of an invasion by Henry Tudor. The Castle was a great strategic location offering expansive views to sea in all directions, but perhaps the King needed to be nearer to the harbour? Staying beside the water would certainly offer good access to shipping and save an awful lot of steep climbs. But where? Many have researched this and although no definitive answer exists the generally accepted view is that he stayed in a house on Sandside in front of the harbour. The house, now a popular restaurant, bears his name and carries a heritage trail plaque on the front wall to commemorate the King's "reputed" residency here. The truth is that no-one knows for sure, but this building seems the most likely, especially given that it was believed to be owned by Thomas Sage, the wealthiest ship owner in Scarborough at the time and well known for his support of the King.

A final thought. Henry Tudor went on to defeat Richard at the Battle of Bosworth the following year. Had he not, Scarborough might not even feature in this guide. Why not? A few months before his death, Richard had produced and sealed a Charter for Scarborough, which, amongst other things, would have effectively made Scarborough a county in its own right. Henry VII as he became, refused to recognise the charter so it was never enacted, and Scarborough remained in Yorkshire.

Further Reading

The Scarborough Book of Days, Robert Woodhouse, The History Press (2013)

Scarborough Through Time, Mike Hitches, Amberley Publishing (2011)

R is for Railways

What becomes of disused railway lines? To be fair, sometimes nothing, but often a line that once carried thousands of visitors to the coast every year is transformed into an attraction that will continue to draw new visitors to the same region.

Map 33: The old railway line between Scarborough and Cloughton

https://www.google.com/maps/d/edit?mid=zR-wiCMof9PQ.kfBmNs9o8GRw&usp=sharing

Map 34: Larpool Viaduct between Whitby and the village of Hawsker

https://www.google.com/maps/d/edit?mid=zR-wiCMof9PQ.kZE5b7rf-0xo&usp=sharing

Map 35: The old Hull – Withernsea railway line

https://www.google.com/maps/d/edit?mid=zR-wiCMof9PQ.ki8pWCQl076A&usp=sharing

There are many that would argue it is the railways that brought tourism to the Yorkshire Coast. It cannot be denied that hundreds of thousands of Victorian visitors flocked to Scarborough, Whitby, Filey and the like every summer once a regular steam railway service became available. However, the railways also helped to finish off many established industries along the Yorkshire coastline. For example, Bridlington gained tourists but lost much of its harbour trade within 15 years of being connected to the rail network (See P for Piers, Pierrots and Promenades). On the other hand, coastal towns such as Withernsea owe their continued existence to the railways.

Withernsea, like so much of the Holderness coast has suffered from erosion for millennia. The coastline at Withernsea is over half a mile inland of where it was a few hundred years ago. Before the railway line connected Hull with Withernsea in 1854, the resident population of the town was just over 100. Within 50 years this had increased tenfold, and by 1920, arguably when Withernsea "peaked" as a tourist destination the town had over 4,500 permanent residents. The importance of a rail connection between Hull and Withernsea was highlighted by a reporter for the *Hull Packet* Newspaper who wrote on the occasion of the line's opening in June 1854:

"Less than twelve months ago we visited Withernsea for the first time, having walked some miles from the extreme point from Hull at which the coach had set us down, there being no conveyance to Withernsea. "

The reporter continued by describing in graphic detail the challenges involved in journeying from Hull to Withernsea by horse and carriage:

"The journey was then necessarily one of two or three hours, accomplished over a dusty road by three re-lays of horses, and not without change of carriage. It was no mean performance to convey two dozen passengers, inside, outside, on dickey, in the basket, and rolling on the roof among boxes, baskets, straps, iron rods, great coats, tarpauling and miscellaneous things."

The new 18-mile railway line clearly impressed the reporter who noted:

"a thousand people can now be walking the busy streets of Hull at one end of the railway, and within that very same hour be pacing the strand on the sea beach of Withernsea".

Thousands would have read the rave review, even tucked away on page 6 of the newspaper. In spite of the unfinished hotel and the failure to provide a single bathing machine the conclusion was glowing:

"the scene was one of beauty which it would defy the power of any painter fully to imitate".

The line was an instant success, carrying 1032 passengers between Hull and Withernsea in its first three operational days. A month later, the same newspaper reported that 700 passengers were travelling every day and queues of 200 passengers had been seen at the ticket office in Hull.

In August of the same year one of several regular charitable events took place, as printed in the *Suffolk Chronicle* under the somewhat inappropriate headline of

CHEAP TRIP FOR LUNATICS

It seemed that the York and North Midland, and Hull and Holderness railway companies had offered free passage to a party of 60 male and female patients from the Hull Borough Asylum so that they could enjoy a supervised day out at Withernsea. Apparently the train ride to the seaside was *"enlivened by the exhilarating strains of the violin"* which the paper revealed was *"played by a lunatic"*. A dinner, served on the beach, comprised *"excellent beef and bread, ale and fruit pies"* and *"a little of the 'weed' for the male portion"*. By all accounts, a grand day was had by all.

Return fares when the service commenced started at 1 shilling per passenger, rising to 2 shillings for first class travel. With three trains a day in each direction, revenues quickly mounted up. Figures were published stating that profits in excess of £25 per day was commonplace.

Natural erosion doesn't stop for tourists though, so the need for sea defences became urgent. Between 1900 and 1960 sea defences stretching for a mile and a quarter were installed. When constructing sea walls for environmental purposes, little is added to the cost if promenades are laid out simultaneously. Visitors not tempted to bathe could always stroll along the promenade without the inconvenience of wet sand from a beach walk. Therefore, Withernsea would not exist as we know it today if it wasn't for the railway line. Sadly, by 1950, traveller's preferences had changed to the point that profits had not only been eroded away completely but that on Sundays, for example, total ticket receipts could be as little as £8. With daily running costs of £83, the Sunday service was deemed unsustainable. Within fifteen years the line had closed for good.

At the peak of the railways more and more visitors flocked to the coast, with the consequence that new industries were created while many others expanded rapidly. Tourists had money to spend, so entrepreneurs found ways to take their money off them. Take the trade in Jet at Whitby, for example. The Whitby and Pickering Railway began operating regular services in 1836. At the time the number of people registered as "Jet

Workers" was 15. Within 35 years this had risen to 795. In fact, the population rise for the town almost exactly matched the rise in Jet Workers during this period. As any visitor to Whitby today will observe, there is no shortage of Jet Workers in the town to this day.

Scarborough saw its population more than double (from 13,000 to over 30,000) in 50 years after the York and North Midland Railway opened a regular line connecting Hull to the town in 1845.

The town of Saltburn-by-the-Sea probably would never have been built at all were it not for the development of railways. The Pease family already had homes in the area. Their mining interests locally would also benefit from rail provision. As stock holders in Railway companies they were well placed to get what they wanted. But Henry Pease had a grander vision. At the time Saltburn was just a small fishing village at the base of the cliffs. Farm land on top of the cliff was in the ownership of Lord Zetland. Pease convinced Lord Zetland to sell a total of 135 acres over a period of 16 years. The first ten acres allowed Pease to build a Railway Station, Hotel and several other buildings. At the time, it was believed to be the first hotel with its own private railway platform. Saltburn now is a town of some 6,000 residents, that number rising significantly during the summer season.

Eventually the Railway system served pretty much everywhere along the coast. Staithes, for example got its own station (on the Whitby, Redcar and Middleborough Union Railway) in 1883. The line has long gone, but if you look closely as you walk around the tiny village, you will see that the station itself still exists. To reach the village, trains had to cross the Staithes Viaduct – built in 1875 from concrete and iron. Passengers were afforded spectacular views as they crossed the 790-foot viaduct at a height of up to 150 feet above the valley but it was a fragile structure. A speed limit of 20 mph was imposed on breezy days and when winds got up trains were not allowed to cross the viaduct at all. The line closed permanently in 1958 with the viaduct being demolished two years later.

One viaduct that remains intact is at Larpool on the outer fringes of Whitby. The viaduct carries a single railway track over the Esk Valley and is an amazing feat of Victorian engineering. Built using an estimated five million red bricks, the thirteen spans and twelve legs hold the railway line

120 feet above the river. Wondering what five million bricks looks like? Well, that is roughly enough for 500 large homes – or enough to build ten full-size copies of Buckingham Palace, for example. Construction of such a large viaduct was not without risks. Not one workman died, but in November 1884 one bricklayer had a very lucky escape. The *Whitby Gazette* told his story:

"Early on Friday morning, whilst John Nicholson, Bricklayer, was engaged in filling in some scaffolding holes on the third pillar from the end of the Esk viaduct he overbalanced himself, and fell to the ground a distance of about thirty feet. He was conveyed home to Haggersgate (in Whitby, besides the Esk Estuary), *where Dr. Tinley attended him, and it is hoped his injuries are not serious, apart from a severe shaking and some cuts about the head."*

Just two months earlier, another man had fallen almost 60 feet from scaffolding and in spite of having *"broken one of his legs and (being) shockingly injured about the face and head"*, under the care of Dr. Tinley, the young man also survived. The doctor unfortunately didn't fare so well. He succumbed to an attack of angina at just 55 years old.

Most of the coastal railway services are now just a memory. Many of those that hadn't closed already fell victim to the Beeching Report recommendations in 1965. By then holidaymakers had alternative forms of transport available – and cheaper alternative holiday venues abroad to think about. The challenge for the Yorkshire Coast in the 21st century is to find new ways to appeal to visitors – with or without the railways.

Further Reading

Hand-book to the Hull and Withernsea Railway, Thomas Tindall Wildridge, Barnwell (1884)

Esk Valley Railway Through Time, Alan Whitworth, Amberley (2011)

Scarborough & Whitby Railway Through Time, Robin Lidster, Amberley (2010)

S is for Schhh! Quiet corners of the Yorkshire Coast

Some of Yorkshire's seaside towns attract so many visitors as to feel rather crowded at times. Take Whitby, for example. The town has a permanent population of around 12,000 but has, on average, over 4,000 visitors every day. On the busiest days, the town will have more visitors than residents. The Yorkshire coastline is almost 70 miles long so you'd expect to be able to find a few quieter places to visit. Here are three suggestions.

Map 36: The Village of Holmpton – two chilling tales

https://www.google.com/maps/d/edit?mid=zR-wiCMof9PQ.kRvgIVc-ws-c&usp=sharing

Map 37: Cattersty Sands and Skinningrove

https://www.google.com/maps/d/edit?mid=zR-wiCMof9PQ.k_JJgnQSVvXs&usp=sharing

Map 38: A grave discovery: A peaceful secret garden in a lively seaside town

https://www.google.com/maps/d/edit?mid=zR-wiCMof9PQ.knLkoGj4jnrw&usp=sharing

Some places wouldn't be the same if packed with tourists. RAF Holmpton is one such place – a victim of its own success. This former RAF cold-war bunker was forced to close recently in order to undergo an extensive re-design. Prospective visitors were being turned away on busy summer days. Now it can manage far greater numbers. When you enter the Guardroom, a building of similar size and shape to a Dormer Bungalow you really would not think you were stepping inside the largest nuclear bunker of its type in the United Kingdom.

At the beginning of the 1950's the UK government invested heavily in early warning radar technology and saw the need to make such facilities as attack-proof as possible. The problem was that nuclear weapons attacks were almost impossible to defend against unless you built underground. The result – the ROTOR Radar Defence Programme. Beneath the Guardroom – actually about 120 feet beneath – is a 35,000 square foot command bunker. To help you appreciate the scale imagine digging a hole the size of half of a football pitch so deep that you could stand eight double-decker buses on top of one another below the ground. The structure is encased in a 10 feet thick tungsten reinforced concrete shell, with additional reinforcement provided by brickwork and a waterproof pitch membrane. Between the bunker and the ground is an additional concrete slab designed to protect the bunker from a nuclear blast directly overhead. The whole construction sits on a 20-foot layer of shock-absorbing shale. Visiting the bunker is an eerie experience, especially if and when the guide turns out the electric lights for a moment. Even this structure would not have withstood a targeted missile strike. Does this explain why the bunker contains a hospital and mortuary?

Why build an early-warning station in the middle of nowhere? Three factors determine location. Firstly, the 120 or so stations needed to be spaced out so as to afford total protection of the coastline. Secondly, the altitude was a factor – the higher the location, the further the range. Holmpton is 86 feet above sea level. Finally, locations needed to be away from other sources of electronic interference, such as centres of population and heavy industry. Holmpton ticked all the boxes.

As you might expect, the government were somewhat cagey about what the site would be used for when the original proposal to purchase the land was made. In October 1950, several newspapers announced that plans had been *"deposited for public inspection"* in a number of local council buildings. Those interested parties, perhaps curious as to what lay inside Command Paper 7278 *"Needs of the Armed Forces for Training and Other Purposes"* and other deposited documents, were given a whole fortnight to find them, consider them and offer a response to the proposals. It was *"other purposes"* that the ministry wanted to keep hush-hush about.

Until the late 1980's the threat of nuclear strikes from the Soviet Union was perceived to be very real. It is a chilling thought that the 100 or so weapons targeted on the UK's major towns and cities could have killed three quarters of the population – instantly. Missiles launched in Russia would take 9 minutes to reach their target. The so-called four-minute warning being the time remaining after an allowance of five minutes to confirm the data suggesting an imminent attack.

The tiny village of Holmpton had an earlier, tragic, association with the Royal Air Force. In January 1942, an Avro Manchester bomber belonging to 207 Squadron took off from RAF Bottesford in Leicestershire intending to attack shipyards in Hamburg. Technical problems delayed the flight resulting in the bomber flying out over the North Sea some distance behind the rest of the attack squadron. It was not unusual for this to happen – the Manchester had a history of engine failures, some 25% of them ending up crashing as a result. Flight L7253 was not destined to bomb Hamburg that night. Just over three hours later the plane was seen in flames shortly before crashing and exploding on Mill Hill to the South of Holmpton. All seven crew members lost their lives. A memorial plaque and information board were dedicated in Holmpton churchyard in November 2009.

Cattersty Sands is a beautiful place to visit – all the more so as it doesn't attract large numbers. From the village of Skinningrove, the beach at Cattersty Sands is just a few minutes walk away. Sands stretch out between the jetty at Skinningrove and the cliffs below Warsett Hill. As beaches go, Cattersty Sands seems to have everything. A wide flat section for the sea to wash over, and a more sharply graduated foreshore, where the sand remains dry save for the stormiest spring tides. With sand dunes, cliffs and rock pools to explore, there really is something for everyone here.

Skinningrove was the site of the very first Cleveland (or North Yorkshire, depending on your preference) Ironstone mine when it opened for business in 1848. It was something of a chance discovery. Samuel Frederick Okey was picking up loose pieces of ironstone on the beach at Cattersty when a farmer by the name of Anthony Maynard approached him. Maynard showed Okey some rock fragments and asked Okey to identify them. Immediately Okey recognised Ironstone and enquired as to where Maynard had found it. To his surprise Maynard disclosed that it was all over his farm. Okey accompanied Maynard back to his farm where it emerged that a rich seam of Ironstone was literally running through Maynard's land. Okey immediately drew up an agreement with the farmer so that Maynard would receive sixpence per ton of ironstone mined. James Burlinson was contracted to run the mine and pay the agreed fee – Okey himself being too busy to take on such a large operation.

A year later, for some inexplicable reason Burlinson wanted out of the agreement. His price apparently was just "a glass of brandy and some water". The purchasers happily gave Burlinson an extra brandy! With the rapid expansion of the railways, the demand for iron took off and the mine at Skinningrove operated until 1958.

Mining began in earnest in 1848. A jetty was constructed soon after and horses hauled trucks along a short railway track to the boats waiting to take the ironstone to Middlesbrough. At its peak the mine produced a quarter of a million tons of ironstone each year and employed nearly 1000 men.

During the boom years of the 1850's and 1860's men and their families flocked to North Yorkshire and Teesside to work in the rapidly expanding iron industry. More than 80 different mines were established as the railways fuelled the demand for iron and then gave the mines a rapid and cheap way of transporting it. Middlesbrough grew from a village with 40 inhabitants in 1829 to a thriving town on the Tees, the "Steel river" with a population of over 40,000 just 40 years later.

Most of those who worked at the mine in Skinningrove lived away from the village. In the early 1870's Wilson's Imperial Gazetteer of England and Wales revealed Skinningrove to be "a township in Brotton parish, N. R. Yorkshire; on the coast, 7½ miles NE by E of Guisbrough. Acres, 171. Real property, £225. Population, 86. Houses, 16."

In 1874 the Loftus Iron Company installed a pair of blast furnaces on the cliff top to the west of Skinningrove Beck. In so doing they started a major iron works that would operate for a hundred years. When the

Skinningrove Iron Company took over operations in 1880, the main market for its iron was in Scotland. A rail line was available, but prices were high, so in 1882 work started on a jetty. It took six years before ships were able to dock and be loaded. It soon emerged that the jetty was not long enough to be used effectively so another 40 feet was added by 1891. Skinningrove Jetty had fallen into a state of disrepair in recent times – a century or so of battering tides, a couple of collisions with ships and the military attempting to blow it up in World War II had all contributed to leaving it looking a bit sorry for itself. In 2015 a major project to reinforce the jetty took place, ostensibly to protect the village from flood tides, but additionally to re-open the jetty for visitors.

Should you have family connections with the ironstone mining industry then a trip to the Cleveland Ironstone Mining Museum at Skinningrove is essential. There you will find the full story of mining in the region as well as the opportunity to take a look below ground since the museum is built on the site of the original mine.

Legend has it that Skinningrove was once visited by a merman. In the 1846 publication *The History and Antiquities of Cleveland* it was reported that villagers had in 1607 *"caught a sea-man, who lived upon raw fish for some days"* before making his escape. Fisherman apparently feared to set sail, often hearing groaning noises from the sea similar to that of the merman who *"instead of voice, he shreaked"*. A mosaic merman was recently added to the wall of the Riverside Building in Skinningrove, and further accounts can be read in the museum.

While Cattersty offers peace and solitude, Scarborough with its many thousands of visitors every day during the summer months may not be the first place you'd think of for a quiet day out, but if you are looking for a chance to enjoy some tranquility whilst there, a "secret garden" is well worth hunting down.

Hidden until recently, the Secret Garden was originally built in 1872, inside what was then known as New Cemetery, now Manor Road Cemetery by the superintendent of Scarborough Cemetery, Leonard Thompson. News of the New Cemetery travelled a long way. The *Sheffield Daily Telegraph*, in covering the first interment in July 1872 described a *"very picturesque site"*, *"capable of admitting about 12,000 interments"*.

Adding that *"its slopes and terraces are beautifully laid out in beds and borders of flowers"*. Edward Leppington, a 36-year-old married local cab driver, originally from Hunmanby, near Filey, had the honour of being the cemetery's first burial, although I doubt when he was falling from his cab some three weeks earlier the prospect of making the newspapers was going through his mind.

The "new" cemetery became immediately popular for funerals AND *"as a place of resort"*, being *"much frequented, especially on a Sunday afternoon"* wrote Joseph Brogden Baker in his 1882 *History of Scarborough*. Which may or may not have been in line with Thompson's initial vision. Thompson created the Secret Garden in a part of the cemetery unsuitable for burials, thinking it would serve as a place for contemplation. Features of the garden included a fountain, a pond, winding stairways and paths linking rockeries, shrubberies and alpine gardens as well as a varied selection of trees not normally considered native to the area.

 Only a stone gate post marking the entrance served as a reminder of this once magnificent folly until a group of volunteers, the "friends of Dean Road and Manor Road Cemeteries" took on the task of coordinating its restoration. The local council undertook to clear the overgrown site in 2010 and two years later with the help of a £50,000 grant from the Heritage Lottery Fund, the "friends" group proudly opened the rejuvenated garden to the public.

Now the secret garden is popular once again with young and old alike. Children can follow a trail of robin marker posts from Dean Road Mortuary Chapel all the way into the garden area where benching provided by a grant from the NatWest Community Fund offers those in need of a rest chance to sit down for a while.

For those wanting to take in a longer walk, a path from the Northern end of the Manor Road Cemetery (near to the war graves) connects the secret garden with Peasholm Park by means of the Peasholm Glen trail through a wooded area beside Peasholm Beck.

Further Reading

RAF Holmpton Official Guide, RAF Holmpton Preservation Society (2010)

John Walker Ord, The History and Antiquities of Cleveland, Simpkin, Marshall & Co (1846)

http://www.scarboroughcemeteries.co.uk/

T is for Thankful Villages

Thousands of holidaymakers stay in one of the many "villages" at Cayton Bay, yet many of them won't be aware of the existence of Cayton village, just half a mile inland. The "bay" has provided career opportunities for local people over the years, but the expansion of holiday parks offering every possible facility for visitors has led in recent years to the demise of several Cayton village attractions. Don't let that prevent you from enjoying an excursion to this delightful Yorkshire village.

Map 39: A short tour of Cayton

https://www.google.com/maps/d/edit?mid=zR-wiCMof9PQ.kRjw-pvCKSbU&usp=sharing

Arthur Mee first coined the expression *"thankful village"* in the 1930's when he published King's England. In it he claimed that 31 villages in England were truly thankful, in that every man of the village who went off to war, actually came home again alive. In his reference to the thankful village of Catwick in East Yorkshire he wrote *"Thirty men went from Catwick to the Great War and thirty came back, though one left an arm behind."* Modern research facilities have led to some changes to Mee's original list. Now, 40 of the 16,000 or so villages of England are recognised as being thankful. The village of Cayton, some four miles South of Scarborough is the only thankful village on the Yorkshire coast. An alternative definition is that a village can be declared thankful if it does not have a war memorial. However, this has to be used with caution – as you will see if you take a few minutes to look at the website link below.

There are some who doubt Cayton's claims giving the deaths of two soldiers as being possibly from Cayton. The official list of UK Soldiers killed in the Great War includes Private James William Hinsley of the 4th Special Reserve Battalion, part of the South Staffordshire Regiment. Although Hinsley was born in Attleborough, Norfolk, his official residence was given as Cayton. Private Hinsley was killed in action in April 1918 at the age of

19 and is buried in La Kreule Military Cemetery in Hazebrouck, northern France. He had been born into a farming family, but as a child the family moved to North Yorkshire around 1903. In 1911, he was living at Carr Farm, Lebberston – half way between Filey and Cayton. Lebberston is a village in its own right so the sad death of Private Hinsley does not prevent Cayton from being a thankful village.

A second soldier quoted by some as being a Cayton resident was Private Thomas William Peacock, 1st Battalion Loyal North Lancashire Regiment. He died ("*accidentally killed*" according to the official Register of Effects) during the Somme campaign in September 1916. Private Peacock had been raised in Scarborough, but was registered with the Ministry of War as being a resident of Cayton Bay, a separate community a little over half a mile to the North-East of Cayton village.

Regardless the criteria used to determine a village's eligibility for thankful status, it is remarkable that Cayton sent over 40 men to war and all of them returned. Of all the thankful villages in England, only Upper Slaughter in the Cotswolds and Arkholme in Lancashire sent more. The UK population was reduced by nearly 2% as a result of almost a million military deaths between 1914 and 1918. A further 3% returned wounded, although this figure does not include countless thousands of men, young and old, who suffering from shellshock - what we now call Post Traumatic Stress Disorder.

Remarkably, all the men of Cayton who fought in the second world war also came home. As a result, the villagers raised funds to commemorate this very fortunate double achievement. In 1947 Potts of Leeds were commissioned to install a new clock in the tower of the parish church of St. John the Baptist. Should you visit, take a walk around the outside of the church and keep your eyes close to the floor. In a corner, between two drain pipes if you look carefully you will spot a rather different timekeeping device – a scratch dial. Sometimes called mass clocks, this one is likely to be in a different position to its original placement as these are more normally sighted much higher up. Since the church dates back to Norman times and mechanical clocks tended to be commonplace by the fifteenth century it can reasonably be assumed that this sundial is over 600 years old.

The concept of "standard time" is a relatively recent one. Greenwich Mean Time was only adopted as a single standard time across the United Kingdom in 1880, and then only in response to demands from the railway companies. If it was 4 o'clock in one town and quarter past 4 in a neighbouring town, train timetables could become very confusing. Probably not much of an issue for the 450 or so residents of Cayton in the nineteenth century with only a single train a day calling in between Scarborough and Hull. The Greenwich Meridian Line, by the way, crosses the Yorkshire Coast just to the north of Withernsea. A marker post that once stood on the cliff top near Tunstall is now in pieces on the beach – a reminder of the fragility of this wonderful coastline.

Yorkshire has four more thankful villages, besides Cayton and Catwick. Cundall, south of Thirsk and Norton-Le-Clay, a mile to the south west of Cundall, Helperthorpe, between Malton and Flamborough and finally, the village of Scruton, to the west of Northallerton. Two more Yorkshire villages, Welbury and Coverham have claimed to be thankful in the past, but some contrary evidence has led to uncertainty.

Further Reading

For more information about thankful villages in general:
http://www.hellfirecorner.co.uk/thankful.htm

Arthur Mee, Enchanted Land, Hodder & Stoughton (1951)

U is for Ups and Downs

Map 40: A walking tour of Robin Hood's Bay

https://www.google.com/maps/d/edit?mid=zR-wiCMof9PQ.kY6jpOSmXJa0&usp=sharing

Map 41: A hill-climb overlooking Scarborough

https://www.google.com/maps/d/edit?mid=zR-wiCMof9PQ.kX7lvsfV7Xn8&usp=sharing

There are plenty of places on the Yorkshire coastline where visitors can almost step out of the car, off the bus or train and be on the beach. Bridlington, Hornsea and Scarborough for example. A few places require a bit more of an effort. In the case of Robin Hood's Bay, a lot more of an effort.

First it is probably best to deal with the name of the place. Robin Hood's Bay has no proven connection with Robin Hood. There is no more evidence the green-tighted one ever went there than there is that he wore green tights. However, there is an old English ballad in which Robin Hood forces French pirates to surrender their treasure which he subsequently hands over to the poor of Robin Hood's Bay, but this is no more than a folk tale. What is known is that a settlement by the name of Robin Hoode Baye was recorded in 1536 at which time it was a major port, probably bigger than Whitby.

The geography of Robin Hood's Bay is complex. The main thoroughfare, New Road follows a steep descent alongside King's Beck down to the sea. The Beck disappears beneath housing for a while before emptying directly onto the beach. Abrupt cliffs rise up to either side of the settlement.

The Cleveland Way passes through the village and *Wainwright's Coast to Coast Walk* has its eastern terminus here so it has a steady flow of passers-through as well as holidaymakers.

It is a place of remarkable natural beauty as well as a place of galleries, tearooms, book shops and antiques stores. In short, there is nothing not to like about Robin Hood's Bay. There was, however, once, one un-named person who took a very obvious dislike to the place, with sinister results. Between 1928 and 1948 at least 600 of the 800 or so population of Robin Hood's Bay received one or more anonymous poison pen letters. The letters falsely accused and exposed members of the population causing untold distress to many. It was rumoured that some people moved away to escape the slanderous letters – at least one vicar amongst them. It took a priest to read out one of the letters in full to his congregation for the full extent of the situation to be revealed. A subsequent police and forensic investigation led to a suspect being interviewed but never charged. The letters stopped but the mystery remains unsolved.

More than 100 years earlier the writer of an 1825 Scarborough Guide described Robin Hood's Bay as having a *"grotesque appearance"*. He added *"The road is by no means good for carriages, on this account therefore and also from its distance, it is usually visited by gentlemen only"*. Thankfully, the accepted view these days is that Robin Hood's Bay is anything but grotesque and is visited by both genders in similar numbers.

Newspaper advertisements from the period reveal that the cost of a carriage ride from Whitby or Scarborough to Robin Hood's Bay was 10 shillings each way – a week's wages for many.

The 1825 guide did give an insight into the main industry of Robin Hood's Bay at the time – fishing. The author wrote *"The quantity of fish which is dried at Robin Hoods Bay, as well for home consumption as for exportation, is surprising. The fronts of its houses and the surface of its paddocks are often covered by them as they are spread to dry"*. It wasn't just the amount of fish landed that was surprising. Fishing boats often travelled hundreds of miles in search of a good catch as The Times newspaper reported in 1803:

"The fishing boats of Staithes, Robin Hoods Bay, and Filey have been this year uncommonly successful in the herring fishery off Yarmouth, having taken from 20 to 25 lasts".

Given that a *last* of herrings is ten thousand fish, this amounts to a quarter of a million herring – well worth sailing down to the East Anglian coast for. As with so many coastal communities the arrival of the railways (here in 1885) brought about rapid change. By the onset of the First World War, only two full-time fishing boats were still operating out of Robin Hood's Bay.

A few years after this first guide book, John Cole produced an updated version for the same publisher. In this guide he revealed that visitors arriving by carriage from Scarborough and the South had a different route available to the one used by road vehicles these days:

"The road ... to ... Robin Hood's Bay is along the sandy beach, close under a high steep cliff, to which the sea flows as the tide advances, and the passage is unsafe, except there be a spacious area of the sand uncovered by the water, or the tide be receding."

Perhaps in response to criticism of the previous editions use of the word *grotesque*, Cole, repeated the term, but qualified it as part of a description of the effects of coastal erosion on the village. He wrote:

"The village consists of the habitations of fishermen and once made a grotesque appearance, the houses being strangely scattered over the face of a steep cliff, and some of them hanging in an awful manner on the projecting ledges of the precipice; but this place has lately sustained a great alteration by the falling of the cliff; in consequence of which, the projecting houses and the pavement of the principal street as far as the fronts of the houses on the opposite side, are ruined and a new road has been made from the landing place through the interior part of the town."

Cole used the word *town* and *village*. Which is more appropriate now? Given that Robin Hood's Bay has lost over 200 buildings as a result of erosion and storm damage, perhaps it was once a town but is now a large village. In 1888, The Whitby Gazette printed a photograph taken by Frank M Sutcliffe showing the slipway and Bay Hotel looking remarkably similar to its present day appearance, but in the background looking North, buildings unprotected from the tides are shown in a precarious state. An immense sea wall, completed in the 1970's restricts further advances, but at the time of writing, this is now in need of considerable reinforcement.

There can be no doubts about Scarborough – this is definitely a town and a large one at that, with a permanent resident population in excess of 60,000 people. Most visitors will be familiar with the town's famous ascent to the Castle and the grave of Anne Brontë, but unless you have a passion for motorcycles you may not have come across the other one – Oliver's Mount.

Joseph Mallard William Turner probably knew of it. He painted several seascapes from the water's edge as well as sketching a mill and the castle from unidentified viewpoints to the south of the town. To appreciate fully the locations possibilities, he almost certainly ascended the hill that was then known more popularly as Weaponness.

Why Oliver's Mount? Apparently Oliver Cromwell, although there is no evidence that Cromwell ever came to Scarborough some historians believe that at the time of the Civil War he did have guns positioned on the hill. Broadrick's New Scarborough Guide (in 1811) gave more details:

"A considerable addition has been lately made to the accommodations for public exercise. The Corporation have inclosed Weaponness Hill, or Mount Oliver: the latter name is acquired from a mistaken opinion of it's having been the scite (sic) from which the parliamentary forces battered the church and castle, during our unhappy divisions in the seventeenth century."

The guide added:

"A driving road is made round the hill, winding to a fine level plain on it's top, whence the view   is very extensive."

The word *extensive* doesn't really do it justice. On a clear day Whitby is visible to the North and Flamborough Head to the South with fine views of Cayton Bay, Filey and Robin Hood's Bay as well as inland.

Nowadays Oliver's Mount is a regular venue for motorcycle racing. It's challenging twisty 2-and-a-half-mile street track draws in some of the best riders and very large crowds. Car races also take place here every year, so if you are looking for a quiet place to walk and admire the view, it is probably best to plan ahead – busy race weekends can attract crowds of up to 60,000 people onto the hill. If racing is not on the agenda when you visit, the circuit makes for a good walk and incorporates a café at the side of the road.

For those inclined to walk a little further, the 16 acre mere sits immediately below Oliver's Mount to the South-West. It has been popular with anglers for well over a century. As long ago as 1896 the Scarborough Corporation stocked it with *"1000 roach, 1000 perch and 250 king carp ... brought in tanks from Caiston, in Lincolnshire"*. Unfortunately, the report in the *Hull Daily Mail* misspelt the Lincolnshire town of Caistor, but did accurately quote the total cost at £30. At today's prices the carp alone would cost at least 200 times this amount. In recent years the Mere has been allowed to revert back to a natural haven for wildlife and to look at it now you'd struggle to believe this was once a popular tourist destination with boat rides, a café and even a pirate ship taking children out on an island adventure. Theakston's Guide to Scarborough somewhat unfairly described the mere in 1853 as:

"possessing no attraction beyond the pleasant walk along its margin"

Trust me, if you tour the mere's margins today, you won't be disappointed.

Further Reading

The Scarborough Guide, Longman & Co. (1825)

John Cole, The Scarborough Guide, Longman & Co. (1829)

A New Scarborough Guide (sixth edition), Broadrick & Co. (1811)

All the above available to read freely online.

V is for Villages on a Headland

The Flamborough Peninsula is not very big, but it certainly packs a punch. Where else can you find two lighthouses, a Grade I listed Georgian country house with over 50 acres of landscaped gardens – plus a zoo, one of the largest accessible seabird colonies in Europe and a scheduled ancient monument that may date back almost as far as Roman times. All within walking distance of one another!

Map 42: A walk to the RSPB site from the twin villages

https://www.google.com/maps/d/edit?mid=zR-wiCMof9PQ.kvam5OFp7yyM&usp=sharing

Map 43: A visit to a house in the country with its own zoo

https://www.google.com/maps/d/edit?mid=zR-wiCMof9PQ.k1FDWhmu608I&usp=sharing

Map 44: Two very different lighthouses

https://www.google.com/maps/d/edit?mid=zR-wiCMof9PQ.kk6v-nghPnsc&usp=sharing

The villages of Bempton (with its close neighbour Buckton), Sewerby and Flamborough sit in a triangle roughly mirroring the shape of Flamborough Peninsula in the East Riding of Yorkshire. Each is worthy of a visit for different reasons. The cliffs at Bempton are homes to some of the finest colonies of seabirds in Europe. Sewerby has a recently renovated stately home and Flamborough village leads to the oldest surviving complete lighthouse in England.

If Bempton and Buckton can be thought of as twins (which is how they like to see things) then Bempton is definitely the bigger of the two, but Buckton is most definitely not the runt of the litter. Most of the 1000 or so population live in Bempton and it is Bempton that comes to mind when thinking about the RSPB reserve, but Buckton, just a few dozen paces to the west of Bempton has a beautiful pond which is often a stopping off point for several different species of migratory birds. Behind the pond are medieval earthworks. Several of these exist and are possibly remnants of the 13th century settlement known variously as Newsham or Newsholm. An information board in the village gives further details. Perhaps Bempton and Buckton should be considered as two of three triplets after all?

The RSPB site caters for all needs. The recently upgraded Grandstand Trail is fully accessible and includes two viewpoints with built-in wheelchair bays. For a change of viewpoint, a nature trail beside the visitors centre passes through long grass and alongside ponds offering opportunities to spot butterflies, moths, dragonflies, rabbits and hares – even the odd deer every once in a while. However, it is the seabird colonies that attract most people to Bempton Cliffs.

Don't worry if you can't tell a razorbill from a fulmar, as well as staff within and (usually) outside the visitor's centre there are usually more than a few twitchers around who are always happy to offer advice. What you can see on and around the cliffs will depend on the time of year that you visit. One species that is an almost ever-present is the gannet. With the exception of September through to January (when they migrate to West Africa), as many as 11,000 pairs of Northern Gannets make their homes on the 120-metre-high cliffs. Possibly the best time to see and photograph these beautiful birds is late spring. During the breeding season their heads and necks become a bright golden-yellow, which together with their bright blue eyes makes them particularly photogenic, especially against a background carpet of red campion flowers. As you watch these majestic birds, whether they are clinging to the same precarious chalk ledge that they call home year on year, or diving for food at over 60 miles per hour or just gracefully gliding on the breeze it is sometimes hard to appreciate that you are looking at a bird the same weight as a small turkey, with a wingspan of over six feet.

Many come to Bempton Cliffs hoping to see Puffins. If you visit between May and July, you shouldn't be disappointed. From the viewing platforms jutting out over the cliff edge you will be able to see them nesting in an assortment of holes and cracks in the chalk and diving for food straight off the cliff face.

Just up the road from Bempton, the Filey Bird and Observatory Group publish an annual bird report. The most up to date issue will set you back around £8, but is an excellent guide to all wildlife in the area – not just birds, and is accompanied with dozens of fantastic photographs. If you shop around in Filey may also find back issues going cheep!

Bempton Cliffs are home to around 220,000 seabirds who do generally get on very well together. True, gannets do often squabble over nest sites, and herring gulls will frequently steal eggs from the nesting guillemots, but, do you know what, if you put a quarter of a million people together in a small open space and forced them to compete for homes and food, I doubt they'd get on any better.

The Yorkshire coastline has always needed defending, so it is no surprise that Bempton has also been a home to the military. RAF Bempton was established in 1940. Remains of a few buildings can be seen just to the north of the RSPB site. Please be aware that the site is on private ground and is in an unsafe condition so if you want to get a good look, there are plenty of websites offering close up photos without the need to risk your life.

RAF Bempton was originally intended as an early warning radar station with its sights firmly on the Luftwaffe. After the war, the perceived threat was a nuclear attack from Russia and so in 1951 the site was rebuilt as part of the ROTOR programme. (RAF Holmpton was part of the same programme and is open to visitors). A little bit like an iceberg, what you can see above ground at Bempton is just a tiny fraction of the facility.

The White Horse Inn, built in the 1930's, was popular with RAF personnel as well as villagers. Although its Blue Dutch tiled roof is a sight to behold and looks remarkably similar to Air Force Blue, it actually attracted complaints from RAF pilots during World War II. Apparently it stood out like a sore thumb from the air and the fear was that German pilots would be able to use it to home in on their base as a target. So for most of the war, the roof was painted over in camouflage colours. As is the case with so many public houses, the White Horse is no longer open for business, but the spectacular blue roof is still well worth seeing.

The RAF base was thankfully never attacked, in war or peacetime, but the deaths of two of its airmen in 1953 serve as a reminder of the dangers of the cliffs nearby. On 11th August *The Yorkshire Post* reported a "**Second Fatality in Two Days**". The newspaper elaborated:

> *"Within an hour of the holding of an inquest at Bridlington last night, on an airman who fell down the cliffs at Bempton, near Bridlington, on Sunday, a second airman fell to his death at the same spot."*

In those days, the cliffs were not fenced off and the airmen believed that it was possible to scramble down to the sea in order to take a swim. Tragically, it took their deaths for a fence to be erected.

A couple of miles to the South of Bempton is Sewerby Hall, a place with its own connection with the Royal Air Force and Aviation. This is a Grade I listed Georgian Country House with over 50 acres of landscaped gardens overlooking Bridlington Bay and much of the Holderness Coast. The Hall was built by John Graeme between 1714 and 1720 and remained in the Graeme family and its descendants for over 200 years. Many improvements and additions were made to the estate during the middle part of the nineteenth century including the Clock Tower, Gatehouse and a large conservatory known as the Orangery. In 1934, the house and much of the estate transferred into public ownership. Bridlington Corporation, the purchasers, immediately determined to open the hall and gardens to visitors. A crowd of 15,000 people turned up on 1st June 1936 to witness the opening ceremony at which, the *Yorkshire Post* stated *"Mrs. Mollison received a great welcome"*. Earlier, the newspaper reported, Mr and Mrs Mollison had attended a reception at Bridlington Town Hall as guests of the mayor Alfred Edward Fligg. So, who was Mrs. Mollison? Perhaps the mayor's introduction helps us. Alderman Fligg described her as *"the greatest airwoman in the world"*, a woman whose *"record had not been equalled"*, and a woman who *"had shown the world what could be achieved, and what the future possibilities were of bringing closer together all the nations of the world."* Only once was her first name mentioned in the report – Amy.

Amy Johnson was born in Hull in 1903 and became famous throughout the world in 1930, when, at the age of 26 she flew solo from England to Australia in just 19 days averaging almost 1000 kilometres every day. In 1932, she married Jim Mollison, another pilot, and promptly celebrated by breaking his own record for a solo flight from London to Capetown, South Africa. She regained this record just three weeks before visiting Sewerby Hall. In May 1936, Mollison completed the flight from Gravesend in Kent in 78 hours and 26 minutes – knocking 11 hours off the existing record time.

Sewerby Hall commemorates this remarkable Aviatrix, as women pilots of the time were known, with an extensive display of memorabilia, gifted by her father in 1958, seventeen years after her untimely death. On 5th January 1941, Johnson (who had reverted to her maiden name after divorcing in 1938) bailed out of an aircraft over the Thames estuary in difficult conditions. She was spotted parachuting into the sea by crew of HMS *Haslemere* whose commander, Lt Cdr Walter Fletcher courageously tried to recover her from the water. Fletcher himself died in hospital shortly afterwards. Amy Johnson's body was never recovered. Two mysteries surround the circumstances of her death. According to official records, Amy was flying alone from Prestwick in Ayrshire, via Blackpool to RAF Kidlington in Oxfordshire yet her plane came down in the Thames Estuary around 100 miles off course. Also several eyewitnesses on board the *Haslemere* reported sighting two bodies in the water. Several theories have been proposed – maybe Johnson was transporting someone on a top secret mission? Also, the "accepted" story is that she must have run out of fuel, but some believe that the plane came down as a result of friendly fire. I doubt that we will ever know.

When you visit Sewerby Hall, you may find it hard to believe that the Orangery, a large glass conservatory was used as a 22-bed convalescent hospital ward for RAF men during the Second World War. The glass roof was covered with felt and a temporary ceiling suspended. Nowadays it is a popular conference and concert venue as well as being used regularly for weddings.

Completing our triangular village tour we travel a couple of miles or so eastwards to Flamborough and Flamborough Head. Larger than Bempton but smaller than the village of Sewerby, at 2,100 it is more than double the size of what it was at the time Victoria took the throne. In his 1828 *Yorkshire Gazetteer*, Stephen Reynolds-Clarke described Flamborough as an *"ancient village, formerly a place of some note ... chiefly inhabited by fishermen"*. He also referred to an *"eminent utility"*, *"on the extreme point of the promontory ... with revolving points"*. He was, of course, writing about the lighthouse. Strictly speaking, Flamborough Head's second lighthouse. Samuel Wyatt's lighthouse was first lit in 1806 and has operated continuously ever since. With a unique pattern of four white flashes every 15 seconds, the lighthouse can be seen up to 24 nautical miles away. It became electronically operated in 1940, was designated a listed building in 1966, and has been unmanned since 1996. Visitors can climb its 27 metre tower which commands excellent views over the sea 65 metres below the cliffs. Joseph Cotton wrote in 1818: *"The scite of Flamborough-head was of all others the most calculated for a lighthouse, either for coasters or for vessels from the Baltic and North Sea, but it was not concurred in by the trade until lately, when its utility having been admitted, the present lighthouse was erected, and the light exhibited upon the principle of the Scilly light, but with coloured red glass in front of the burners, by which it is distinguished from Cromer."*

An earlier lighthouse still stands at Flamborough. Sir John Clayton built a chalk beacon tower between 1669 and 1674. It has since been reinforced with brickwork and is notable for two reasons. Firstly, it is octagonal in shape, and secondly, it was never ever lit. Clayton's intention was to build three lighthouses to serve the area that was notorious for wrecking ships. He hoped to earn a fortune in toll charges but his first (and only) venture bankrupted him and his original commissioner King Charles II refused to provide him with any further financial support.

There is no doubt that the lighthouse will have saved countless lives over its 200+ year time in operation, but shipwrecks still occur on or near to this perilous promontory. In April 1930 for example the Royal Navy Oiling Vessel SS *Rosa* ran aground and was wrecked in heavy seas and thick fog at North Landing. All 16 crew members were successfully rescued by the Flamborough lifeboat which itself suffered some damage in the operation. At low water parts of the wreck including a large section of the steamers boiler can still be seen.

A report in the *Yorkshire Evening Post* the following day helps us to appreciate the danger of working at sea and the bravery of lifeboat crews who take to the waters in all conditions in order to save lives. Apparently warning signals had been fired from the *Rosa* when it first struck rocks at West Scar near to North Landing. Watchers on land alerted the lifeboat men, who readied their craft, Forester, and prepared a rocket line. Crew on the *Rosa* had prepared their own lifeboat, but this was smashed to pieces on the rocks. Thankfully, men on two motorised fishing cobles nearby had warned the *Rosa's* crew that the situation was too dangerous to attempt to board their own boat and to wait for the lifeboat to arrive. The newspaper takes up the story:

"Huge seas were sweeping the vessel from end to end. The lifeboat crew's task was a most dangerous and arduous one. They were between the rolling waves and the rocks. At one time it was feared the lifeboat would be crushed between the vessel and sunken rocks."

In the thirty minutes alongside *"the lifeboat was very much knocked about, and the crew with it"* according to Coxswain Richard Chadwick, who added *"several oars were smashed, but these boats can stand a good deal of hammering."*

This time, all those involved came out of the event largely unscathed. In fact, after drying and warming themselves in front of roaring fires at Ye Olde Thornwick Hotel (now known as The Viking) the inn landlord provided all the survivors with a breakfast and observed all to be *"in pretty good shape."*

Unfortunately, the outcome has not always been positive. On 5th February 1909 the *Yorkshire Evening Post* carried this headline:

SIX FLAMBORO' MEN DROWNED

COBLES CAPSIZED IN A BOILING SEA

The newspaper described how fifteen or sixteen fishing cobles had been caught in a *"windstorm"*, *"one of the most severe"*. In spite of the assistance of both lifeboats and in front of hundreds of anguished onlookers, two boats went down. The result – *"six hale strong fishermen … dashed to death within a stone's reach of the beach."* Eye witnesses reported that on coble, The *Gleaner*, had been struck by a ferocious wave, knocking her three crewmen, John Cross and his sons Richard and Robert into the wild sea. A second coble, The *Two Brothers*, also with a crew of three, Melchior (sometimes recorded as Melchoir) Chadwick, George Gibbon and Tom Leng Major ran alongside and the three Cross family members were pulled aboard. Almost within an instant more enormous waves crashed over the *Two Brothers* throwing all six men into the sea.

Four bodies were recovered quickly. In fact, the funerals of George Gibbon, Tom Leng Major, John Cross and his 17-year-old son Richard took place just three days later. Melchior Chadwick's body was washed up at King and Queen Rocks the following month. The body of Robert Cross was never found.

Later that year a monument was unveiled in Chapel Street, Flamborough, dedicated to the memory of the six villagers and commemorating the heroism of the *Two Brothers* crew. The inscription reads *"Greater love hath no man than this that a man lay down his life for his friends."*

A second memorial stone had to be laid at the same site in 1984, following the deaths of seven more men in stormy seas.

Nowadays, just a single lifeboat based at South Landing serves the whole of this rocky promontory.

Further Reading

The New Yorkshire Gazetteer or Topographical Dictionary, Stephen Reynolds-Clarke, Teesdale & Co (1828)

Memoir on the Origin and Incorporation of the Trinity House of Deptford Strond, Joseph Cotton, Darling, London (1818)

Shipwrecks of the Yorkshire Coast, Arthur Godrey & Peter Lassey, Dalesman (1974)

W is for Wet and Wild

Hornsea Mere dates back to the last ice age while Welwick Saltmarsh only began to form in the last couple of hundred years. Both attract an abundance of wildlife for different reasons and offer visitors a fantastic day out.

Map 45: Welwick Saltmarsh Nature Reserve

https://www.google.com/maps/d/edit?mid=zR-wiCMof9PQ.kQlrZQucfrnM&usp=sharing

Map 46: Hornsea Mere

https://www.google.com/maps/d/edit?mid=zR-wiCMof9PQ.kqxYkj_BBbvY&usp=sharing

The unassuming village of Welwick lies a couple of miles south-east of Patrington but has a surprisingly long and continuous history. Arable farming has been taking place on the land around this settlement since the eighth century. The church of St. Mary at least in part dates back to the late thirteenth century. In fact, anyone looking for a peaceful meander around a delightful country village could do a lot worse than spend an afternoon in Welwick.

However, it is what lies to the south of the village that is the focus of our attention on this occasion. Travel south (on wheels or foot) along Humber Lane and after a couple of miles you will reach a dead end. Welwick and Weeton Banks face you. Behind them is almost 110 acres (about the size of 65 association football pitches or three times the size of Peasholm Park in Scarborough) of saltmarsh. Behind that is the Humber Estuary. Behind that are Cleethorpes and Grimsby in North-East Lincolnshire.

This is one of the best places in Yorkshire to view a variety of raptors hunting freely. Look out for peregrines, kestrels, hen harriers and owls.

The short-eared owl is regularly seen here. A recent addition is a flock of 20 Mule Gimmer Sheep, whose grazing on and around the Saltmarsh is hoped to promote growth and strengthen the natural habitat of the area.

Maintaining this reserve is constantly challenging. You can't have a wetland without a lot of water, but the Humber does get more than its fair share of tidal surges. As recently as December 2013 a spring tide of over 7 metres was boosted by a further 2-metre-high surge, enough to breach defences along the Humber estuary and cause considerable damage to the Welwick Wetland Reserve.

Obviously wetlands are potentially dangerous places to visit, so it is strongly advised that you do not stray from the raised embankments that run along parts of its boundaries. Avoiding encroachment will not only keep you safe, but will preserve the environment in which so many species – animal, bird, insect and fauna – live.

If you are determined to have a more hands-on approach and want to get on the water itself, then a trip north to Hornsea might be just the ticket for you. Here, just half a mile from the coastline is the largest freshwater lake in Yorkshire – Hornsea Mere. Look, it isn't exactly Loch Ness (the Mere is 2 miles long, Loch Ness is 21 miles longer), but compared with Scarborough Mere at 16 acres, Hornsea Mere is around 30 times the size. Perhaps surprisingly for such a large freshwater lake, it has a maximum depth of just 12 feet.

This area of Holderness was covered by a large glacier during the most recent ice age. In places, up to a mile thick and stretching back as far as Scandinavia. As it melted eleven and a half thousand years ago it left behind huge deposits of boulder clay, but dozens of large blocks of ice remained embedded in the clay. Over time as temperatures continued to rise these blocks melted forming seventy or more meres of varying sizes. Smaller ones gradually filled in with clay and ultimately peat so that now only Hornsea Mere remains – a single freshwater legacy of the ice age.

If you fancy a spot of fishing, two words of caution – tickets and pike. You will need to purchase the appropriate ticket first – whether fishing from the shore or from a boat. Also be aware that there are some big fish swimming in the Mere. Carp have been known to reach 50 pounds or more – that's the average weight of a typical seven-year-old boy! Pike are prevalent throughout the Mere and regularly get hauled in with weights of well over 20 pounds. In Joseph Morris's East Riding of Yorkshire guide, the author referenced William Lambert writing in 1693 (using the accepted spellings of the period) on the subject of the Mere's waters:

"... (they are) well replenished with the best pykes, peirches, eles, and other fish; the three named the best and largest that ever I saw or tasted. I have taken pykes a yard long, and peirches sixteen inches"

Please don't be tempted to fish without a ticket. The authorities have a long history of reeling in offenders as this advertisement from the *Hull Packet* newspaper in June 1815 shows:

Hornsea Mere

𝔑𝔬𝔱𝔦𝔠𝔢 𝔦𝔰 𝔥𝔢𝔯𝔢𝔟𝔶 𝔊𝔦𝔳𝔢𝔫

That WHOEVER after the date hereof, shall be detected Fishing, or for any other purpose Trespassing in the above Lake, without leave in writing from the Owner thereof, will be prosecuted as the Law directs.

Proper Persons (to whom for every conviction on their information, the penalty of FIVE POUNDS thereby to be recovered will be given) are appointed to look after and inform of ALL OFFENDERS.

Note that the use of capitals was not added by me – you have been warned!

In the thirteenth century the Mere was the subject of an intense dispute between the abbots of Meaux Abbey and St. Mary's in York who both claimed exclusive rights to fish its waters. When agreement between the two could not be reached, both abbots agreed to a duel to settle the matter. Now, before the vision of a couple of monks fighting gets too well established in your mind I should explain that each abbot hired a knight to duel on his behalf. The outcome? St. Mary's was declared victorious, but a compromise was made allowing representatives from Meaux Abbey to fish the waters anyway.

Standing mereside these days you are unlikely to see any duelling knights but you will almost certainly catch sight of several geese, swans, grebes and the like landing and taking off on the water. If you could have been there during the First World War you would have seen some of the earliest seaplanes using the Mere as part of the UK's air defences against German Zeppelin raids. Flight was still in its infancy and aircraft that could land and take off on water were given a variety of names – flying boats, seaplanes and floatplanes, for example. Prior to the war the Mere had been used for a few passenger flights so the military were well aware that it was a suitable stretch of water. At Kirkholme Point on the Eastern (Hornsea) end of the Mere a natural peninsula provided an ideal location for shore-based facilities and a slipway. Nearby at Killingholme the Royal Naval Air Service had established an air station for land planes, so Hornsea Mere was quickly commandeered into service. Several buildings quickly followed – one of them on Kirkholme Point is still used as headquarters of the local sailing club. Over 140 personnel were stationed in order to operate 12 Sopwith Baby and Short 184 Seaplanes. To give you an idea of the scale, the Baby was nearly 24 feet long, with a wingspan to match – a little bit shorter than a typical minibus, but somewhat wider. The Short 184 was about twice as big and carried a crew of two, whereas the Sopwith Baby was a single seater.

Airmen had to contend with their own machinery as much as the enemy in the First World War. On the final day of February 1918 Flight Lieutenant H C Lemon piloted a Short 184 with Flight Commander P D Robertson in the second seat as observer. Shortly after take-off catastrophic engine failure caused the plane to come down on marshland to the south of the mere. Robertson managed to jump clear as the plane came down, but on seeing the pilot trapped in the burning wreckage he made several attempts to free his colleague and friend. Tragically, he was unsuccessful and suffered severe burns to his face and limbs.

The Imperial War Museum has a recording of a pilot, G F Hyams who flew the Sopwith Baby from Hornsea Mere in the last year of the war. Hyams recalled that each pilot was issued with a box containing a homing pigeon, who he affectionately referred to as "petty officer". In the event of the plane coming down, the idea was to write a note and attach it to the pigeon so that a rescue could be arranged. Apparently this was used to great effect on several occasions – a bit more cumbersome than a mobile phone, but a lifesaver all the same.

Returning to Welwick, the village is associated with three of the conspirators in the gunpowder plot of 1605. Jack and Kit Wright were born in the village, and Guy Fawkes himself apparently often travelled from his home in York to meet his co-conspirators at Potters Barn, part of Plowlands Farm. Fawkes had known Kit Wright since sharing schooldays together in York. A large steel sculpture featuring images of four of the plotters (Robert Catesby being the other) was erected in the village in 2013. Most people will recall the name of Guy Fawkes with the conspiracy to assassinate King James I by detonating gunpowder beneath the House of Lords during the State Opening of Parliament. Catesby, in fact, led the conspirators, but it is Fawkes who is remembered as the man caught red-handed with 36 barrels of gunpowder in his possession. Guy Fawkes was the only one of the four featured in the sculpture to stand trial. Catesby and the Wright brothers took flight, only to be hunted down and killed in a firefight in Staffordshire. As a warning to others, Robert Catesby's body was later exhumed from its grave and his head displayed outside parliament. The fate of Fawkes is well known. As with all those found guilty of treason at the time he was hanged, drawn and quartered.

Other members of the Wright family are commemorated in the village church of St Mary where an unsolved mystery remains. For a start off, the church appears to be quite large for such a small village. Inside is a large tomb, dating back to the fourteenth century bearing a remarkable likeness to the spectacular Percy Tomb inside Beverly Minster almost 30 miles away. Analysts are pretty sure that both tombs must have been crafted by the same people. The Percy Tomb most likely commemorated Eleanor, daughter to the Earl of Arundel. As for the Welwick tomb? Nobody knows for sure. A possible clue is that the tomb, although embedded into the wall of the church, was not always so – in its past life it was probably built to be free-standing. Some have suggested that it was originally situated at Burstall Priory, near Skeffling, just a few miles away. The priory was abandoned more than 300 years ago, and there is evidence that a doorway was salvaged and moved to nearby Easington, so the Welwick Tomb may well have originated there. As to who it was for? Some say, the Earl of Albemarle. Maybe, maybe not. In the twelfth century, Stephen, then the Earl of Albemarle gifted the priory to a group of Benedictine monks, who in turn sold it to the Abbot of Kirkstall in West

Yorkshire two hundred years later. So the timing does not appear to be right for this connection. We may never know for sure – but don't let that stop you taking a look at the tomb and the rest of Welwick village.

Further Reading

The Lost Fens: England's Greatest Ecological Disaster, Ian D Rotherham, History Press (2013)

The Royal Naval Air Service at Hornsea Mere and Killingholme (1914 – 1919), Joe Gelsthorpe, lulu.com (2014)

The East Riding of Yorkshire, Joseph E Morris, Methuen & Co. (1906)

X is for "ten things the Romans did for Filey Bay"

Map 47: Evidence of Roman occupation in and around Filey

https://www.google.com/maps/d/edit?mid=zR-wiCMof9PQ.kBJuMdBYPGH8&usp=sharing

William Smithson Cortis MD, of Queen Street and then John Street, Filey first excavated a Roman Signal Station on Carr Naze, Filey Brigg in 1857 at the request of the local vicar who at the time was owner of the land. As we shall see shortly, he was not the only local doctor with an interest in archaeology. Following a period of heavy rain, a landslip uncovered pieces of wood, a few bones and some pottery. A local painter by the name of Wilson suggested to the Rev. Richard Brooke of St. Oswald's Church that he thought these might be Roman Relics so Brooke asked a number of his associates including the towns medic to investigate. Originally from Hull, Cortis went on to write a guide to Filey in 1866 in which he suggested that the town had very obvious Roman roots. Literature from Roman times often made reference to the East coast bay of *Portus Felix*. Cortis was sure this was Filey as he wrote:

"The name alone is almost sufficient to identify the two; the change to Filey from "Felix," or especially from its genitive or accusative cases, "Filicis" or "Filicem," being comparatively slight."

Filey from Felix or Filicis is quite persuasive to me especially when taken alongside this next point. The Romans retained control of much of England, but not all of it. To the north of Filey along a stretch of coastline the Brigantes continued to rule their roost. On Roman maps this area was marked as "Brigantium Extremum". The boundary line for this region crosses what we now call Filey Brigg.

The Signal Station may never have been discovered were it not for a rapid erosion of the cliff face following heavy rains in August exposing parts of it to the elements for the first time in well over a thousand years. Cortis was able to conduct a full survey of the site and recorded measurements of 50 metres across with foundations for a central square tower measuring some 14 metres square. He postulated that the tower would have been upwards of 30 metres tall. To give a firm base for this tower were five "socket stones". Each one had a three inch deep square "socket" of seven inches across to hold wooden beams, probably of Oak. These have since been relocated and can be seen laid out orientated as they were found in the centre of Filey's Crescent Gardens.

Inscribed on one of the socket stones can be seen:

CAESAR SE

QUAM SPE

Unfortunately the rest is missing, so the translation from Latin into English is not very helpful

Caesar himself

Anticipated

Our good doctor had a further hypothesis concerning the mysteriously carved rocks jutting out from the edge of the Brigg at low tide.

"Somewhat beyond the middle of the Brigg, striking off from its south side at an angle of about 45 degrees, we find the foundation of a pier or breakwater, now called the "spittal rocks", perhaps from hospitium, a shelter. If this work was raised above high water, there would be formed a most excellent harbour for vessels of the size of Roman galleys"

To view the Spittals it is best to visit when the Spring tides are at their strongest so that when the sea is out this mysterious phenomenon is exposed to its maximum. It has been surveyed several times, and the jury is still out I'm afraid. Some believe the breakwater to be a freak of nature while many others argue that its regularity alone prevents it from being anything other than manufactured to serve the needs of shipping.

Cortis led a busy life. As well as providing medical support for the people of Filey and conducting archaeological investigations he published a pamphlet on how to prevent the losses of lives and ships on the north-east coast of England, edited a book on the principles of chemistry and was Captain in charge of the Filey Corps of the 2nd East York Artillery

Volunteers. He married for a second time in 1862 before taking up a position in London. In 1878 he emigrated to Australia, where he remained until his death in 1906. His son William Richard followed him into the medical profession but led the way to Australia six years before his father.

More coins were found at the signal station site in 1862, 1888 and 1909. A rock fall in 1869 also exposed a Roman vase. The noted archaeologist F Gerald Simpson was next to explore Filey's connection with Roman times. Simpson came to Filey Brigg in 1923 with excellent credentials. From 1907 to 1913 he led excavations along Hadrian's Wall in Northumberland and Cumberland whilst still in his twenties for the most part. A year after his studies at Filey he became Director of Field Studies at Durham University, where he was also given an honorary MA in the same year. Simpson studied the Carr Naze site in conjunction with a similar site within the grounds of Scarborough Castle and concluded that the two had been erected at the same time. In fact they form part of a chain of lookout points and beacon sites stretching along the coast between Whitby and Bridlington.

In 1929 Simpson was able to confirm that pottery and bones found sticking out of the exposed cliff face by Percival Travis Clay in 1926 at Gristhorpe Bay just to the north of Filey Brigg (Behind the Blue Dolphin Caravan Park) were in fact remains of a Roman settlement from the same period and suggested another signal station. All traces of this have long since disappeared into the sea below. Coincidentally, Clay had sold his stake in Filey's Crescent Gardens to the Urban District Council in 1920 – he could not have known that several decades later the same council would relocate the five socket stones from the signal station onto an area of land that he had once owned.

William Cortis was not the only doctor in Filey to write a guidebook to the town. The other, *Observations on Filey as a Watering Place*, was published in 1853 by Edward William Pritchard M.D. This man became well-known for all the wrong reasons. Pritchard had doubtful medical credentials, but had served on board the Victory for a while before practicing medicine in Yorkshire. In the 1850's Filey was a very small settlement, and Pritchard ran surgeries there and in Bridlington as well as in his home of Hunmanby. Around 1860 he moved to Glasgow where, five years later he was tried for the murders of his wife and mother-in-law. Examinations of both bodies revealed lethal doses of antimony had been administered. Pritchard was tried, found guilty and hanged in front of a crowd estimated at 80,000 at Glasgow Green. A housemaid had died in a mysterious fire two years earlier and there had been fingers pointed at Pritchard then, but no charges laid. Edward Pritchard has the dubious honour of being the last man to be publicly executed in Glasgow.

Before leaving Yorkshire, the doctor had been actively involved in his own geological surveys. At the same time as Dr Cortis was conducting his research, Pritchard released *On the Discovery of Roman Remains at Filey*, opening his report by describing Filey affectionately as a *"lovely watering place – the rising Brighton of Yorkshire"*.

News of the initial discovery on Carr Naze in 1857 caused much excitement throughout the United Kingdom. The *London Evening Standard* even devoted a full column to the report. Several artefacts were, seemingly quite rare finds. For example, *"a small urn, composed of fine clay, being white with red bars across it"* was found alongside pieces of glass which the newspaper concluded signified the pot as a *feralis urna* with the glass fragments coming from a lachrymatory phial in which the mourner's tears would have been placed to accompany the ashes of the deceased in the urn itself. The material and manufacture of the urn gave a clue as to the wealth or status of the deceased. Earthenware urns were usually used for the less well off, but the fact that the pot was highly decorated with *"beautiful scroll work"* implies a person with some position of relative importance. So perhaps the Romans used Filey for something more than a remote coastal signal station after all?

Another curious artefact was one of the oldest known examples of dentistry. Buried beneath over two feet of earth was exhumed *"a plate for the roof of the mouth, in which was inserted with great skill, an incisor tooth."* The plate itself was carved from animal bone, and the tooth (which would have been a human one) was held in place by two delicate gold rivets. Workmanship the newspaper described as exhibiting *"an amount of skill and neatness that can scarcely be surpassed amongst the moderns."* Several items recovered from a series of archaeological investigations at Carr Naze are in the hands of the Rotunda Museum in

Scarborough. These include a three-foot-high bronze statue of the Roman god Mercury.

There was undoubtedly a significant Roman presence in and around Filey, and we have two very different doctors to acknowledge for much of the work in unearthing (literally) the evidence, both had a great fondness for the town, but one will be remembered for all the wrong reasons.

Further Reading

An Historical and Descriptive Guide to Filey, William Smithson Cortis, Kendall (1866)

A Gazetteer of Roman Remains in East Yorkshire, Mary Kitson Clark (1935)

Y is for Yorkshire's Alum Heritage

What connects the Romans, flocks of sheep, mountains of seaweed, King Henry VIII and barrels of stale urine?

Alum.

Map 48: Ravenscar

https://www.google.com/maps/d/edit?mid=zR-wiCMof9PQ.kXDw4uPaeW0c&usp=sharing

The Romans had long known of the value of Alum – there was plenty of it in Italy. Alum had countless uses, as a leather softener, to staunch the flow of blood, and in paper manufacturing, but the main use for alum was as a mordant, or setting agent, in dying cloth.

Up until the reign of Henry VIII all the alum used in England came from Italy but this supply stopped when the King decided to divorce Catherine of Aragon. The catholic church has never sanctioned divorce and so Pope Clement VII ordered a number of sanctions against England – including banning the export of alum.

The consequence for the cloth industry in England was disastrous. The only way to get fabric dyed was to send it to Flanders, but the quality of Belgian alum was not good so costs increased dramatically at the same time as quality suffered.

Time for Thomas Challoner to make his mark.

Challoner (sometimes spelt Chaloner) was a keen naturalist and traveller. He noted on a visit to Italy that the soil at the papal alum works at Tolfa was very similar to that on his estate at Guisborough. He was particularly interested to observe that leaves all appeared to be a very similar shade of green. When he also discovered fossils very like those abundantly found on the North Yorkshire coast he realised that he was onto something big. What Thomas had quite literally unearthed was that alum was right on his own doorstep.

What Thomas did next led to a papal curse. The production of alum was a closely guarded secret in Italy, so Challoner bribed some of the workers and smuggled them out of the country, concealing them in barrels aboard his boat. He quickly established a business in Guisborough and soon recognised that he needed to expand operations and be nearer to the coast.

Ravenscar was originally known as Peak when Challoner established the Peak Alum Works there. The settlement was renamed in 1897 shortly before plans were made to turn the village into a tourist town to rival nearby Scarborough. Roads were laid, a railway service was installed, sewers were prepared. The Ravenscar Development Company could not be faulted for their ambition. Train loads of prospective investors were brought in from as far away as the Midlands and South East. They must have been impressed by the quality of housing built, and the spectacular views but what Ravenscar could not offer them was easy access to the beach. Ravenscar is perched on a cliff with a perilous 600-foot descent to the sand and rock below. Also, being so high up the village was often shrouded in mist, even during summer months. Even the railway line had issues. Access to the fledgling holiday village was by the steepest ascent in the North East and many trains struggled to cope with the slope. Undeterred, money continued to be invested in the project, but holiday makers stayed away, not tempted by adverts such as this one from the *Leeds Mercury* of 1903:

RAVENSCAR HOUSE
BOARDING HOUSE and PRIVATE
RESIDENTIAL HOTEL
NOW OPEN for RECEPTION of GUESTS
Tea Room,
Also Table d'Hote Luncheons &c.
Specific Catering for Large Parties

Ravenscar House has survived in various forms but the plan to turn Peak village into a "new" Scarborough was always doomed. By 1913 the company had folded and Ravenscar remains to this day a quiet little village with several houseless roads to nowhere.

Alum manufacturing is a complex chemical process and Challoner is rightly regarded as one of the founders of the British chemical industry. The Peak Alum Works looked nothing like a modern-day chemical factory. Hundreds of men quarried grey shale with pickaxes. Bonfires burned for up to nine months until the grey shale turned red. To create a mordant from this burnt alum required the addition of potassium and ammonia. The potassium was readily available as kelp. Seaweed was shipped in from as far away as the Orkney Islands. Ammonia posed a different problem. Human urine had been used in Italy, but with the average man providing only a couple of pints a day, Challoner soon realised that he could not possible get enough urine locally. To get the 200 tonnes per year needed, Challoner had to import barrels of stale urine from the cities of Newcastle and London. By the way, it is believed the expression "taking the p**s" comes from this most unpleasant of trades.

A final curiosity is that someone discovered (we cannot be sure who) that breaking raw eggs until one floated on the surface of the alum solution was the most effective way to assess its readiness.

Alum production in England grew and grew. King James I passed a law effectively banning all imports. England could manufacture high-grade alum cheaper than they could import it anyway, but the message it sent to the Vatican was clear.

Working and living with alum was a risky business. At Kettleness 12 miles further up the coast, alum and iron ore were mined side by side until the cliffs around the iron ore mine collapsed in December 1829. The subsequent landslip led to the destruction of much of the village and the alum works. Fortunately a ship moored offshore was able to rescue most of the residents. Undeterred, the alum works were rebuilt but a fire that burned for two years finished it for good. An eye-witness described the devastation to the *Newcastle Courant* newspaper on 26th December 1829:

"Where only a few short hours before stood a large quantity of buildings, now nothing is to be seen but a few sticks standing in diverse directions

here and there, and the rest one continued mass of the ugly black alum shale."

The scars from the industry are clear for all to see. Cliffs were broken away in the search for good shale, forests were cut down to produce charcoal and poisonous waste tips scorched and killed the natural habitat surrounding the alum works. In 1855, a synthetic method of manufacturing alum was discovered. It soon proved to be much quicker, cheaper and cleaner than the traditional method as it used by-products from towns gas production so the Peak Alum Works along with all of the others fell into decline and finally ceased production in the 1870's.

The National Trust care for the Ravenscar site which is open to the public throughout the year. Remains of the alum industry in Yorkshire can also be seen at Sandsend, Boulby and Lofthouse. For those feeling very energetic an Alum Trail along the Cleveland Way is available online.

But, there is a final positive legacy of this most paradoxical of trades. Quarrying shale from the cliff faces unearthed countless fossilised remains resulting in the Yorkshire coastline becoming a haven for palaeontologists from all over the world.

Further Reading

Burniston to Ravenscar Through Time, Robin Lidster, Amberley Publishing (2013)

The Alum Farm, Robert Bell, Horne and Son (1938)

Z is for Zeppelins over Hull and Hedon

Map 49: The key landmarks of Hull

https://www.google.com/maps/d/edit?mid=zR-wiCMof9PQ.kE_Pee3oT4sc&usp=sharing

Map 50: A visit to Hedon

https://www.google.com/maps/d/edit?mid=zR-wiCMof9PQ.k_4kiiR3XHvE&usp=sharing

OK, so it was arguable whether or not Hull counted as a coastal location. It is a major port on the very wide Humber Estuary, but it does not face the open sea, so I can see both arguments. Whatever you think – it's in!

It may surprise many readers that air raids did not begin in World War II. Many places in Britain endured attacks from the skies in the First World War.

The first air raid resulting in fatalities in Yorkshire came on 2nd May 1916 when York was hit by around eighteen bombs dropped from a Zeppelin airship. Six men and three women lost their lives. Another 40 received treatment for injuries and many homes were destroyed or badly damaged.

Newspapers were restricted on what they could report, so the *Yorkshire Herald* referred to the assault as being on *"a certain place in Yorkshire"*. A week later, Albert Tolchard of Hull was fined £10 (or 51 days' imprisonment if unable to pay) after he *"made a statement in the hearing of several women about Zeppelins which considerably alarmed them"* (*Sheffield Evening Telegraph*, 10th May 1916). Albert, an insurance salesman, had made the mistake of talking about what most people had witnessed. The *Yorkshire Evening Post* described his punishment as *"a warning to gossips"*.

Hull had several of its own Zeppelin raids. On the night of 6th/7th June 1915, Zeppelin L9 diverted to Hull after strong winds prevented it from reaching London. Over a period of 30 minutes either side of midnight it dropped numerous bombs and an estimated 50 incendiary devices on the city. At least 24 civilians died and nearly twice as many homes were destroyed. Kapitanleutnant Heinrich Mathy piloted the L9 and witnessed the devastation in the city and docks. The letter he posted to his wife the following day reveals a conflict of conscience:

"...War is war, they've shot at me and it's a nasty fire, and yet fighting submarines is nicer than setting towns on fire. But we'll always give them all we have, the harder [we attack] the earlier they will crumble..."

Waller Street in East Hull took the first bombs with the destruction of several houses. Clarence Street followed shortly after as Mathy steered his craft too far north of his intended targets in the harbour. Porter Street, Campbell Street, South Parade and East Street were all struck with fatal consequences and a 6 metres by 2 metres crater was the result of a bomb falling on High Street.

In all, Hull was attacked by airships on eight separate occasions – a further 33 civilians died and over 150 were injured. When you consider the city accounted for 10% of all air raid deaths in the First World War when the population of Hull represented well under 1% of the UK population, you can see that Hull was a significant target for the German bombers – even allowing for the two occasions where Hull became a secondary target.

One of the first places to warn of the June 1915 attack was the picturesque little town of Hedon, five miles east of Hull. Major General Ferrier, Commander of the Humber Defences, received at his headquarters in the Royal Station Hotel a report from Hedon at 11.47pm. Almost immediately, the airship was seen over Hull, silhouetted in the clear night sky. Hedon was fortunate that night, but a Zeppelin returned in August 1917 and destroyed the Primitive Methodist Chapel on Baxter Gate. Thankfully all lives were spared. The following day the *Hull Daily Mail* described the scene in Hedon:

"All that remains of the Primitive Methodist Chapel are the four walls, which enclose a great heap of debris. The entire building is gutted, the bomb having smashed the pews, pulpit, and galleries to atoms. Across the way, and within a hundred yards, the Roman Catholic Church suffered

considerably. The frontage of the presbytery, between the church and the
road, has been badly split and shaken: but the church itself has stood the
strain remarkably well. A feature of the interior are six large windows, one
of them being a beautiful memorial in stained glass, and this is the only
one remaining intact. It contain- a fine representation of the Saviour with
the words "Touch me not, for I am not yet ascended to my father"."

This was one of the more detailed newspaper reports to be published. Editors were strongly encouraged (some might say ordered) to minimise the damage done by the German Airship raids. Whenever Zeppelins were repelled, shot down or failed to hit their targets, the newspapers were quick to inform the public. In one account, the *Hull Daily Mail* reported under a headline of **ZEPPELIN FAILURES** that of the *"three bombs … dropped. One failed to explode, and the others between them totally destroyed twenty turnips and made one big hole."* In a final morale-boosting sentence, the paper added *"There were no other casualties"*. Of course, those who lost loved ones and/or their homes knew what was really going on.

If it is debatable whether or not Hull counts as a coastal venue, then the position for Hedon is even murkier. The town is not even mentioned in the Domesday Book but by the thirteenth century had grown to the extent that it was one of the largest ports in England. You wouldn't believe it now, of course. The silting up of the waterway combined with the growth of Hull as a major port means that few visible signs remain that this was ever a bustling centre for the export of wool. Heading up the *Hedon Haven* from the Humber, as the river enters the town it takes on the rather less romantic name of *Burstwick Drain* – but don't let that put you off visiting this lovely place.

Several Zeppelins were shot down over the North Sea and mainland Europe but the only time the people of Hull witnessed an airship coming down happened three years after the end of the war. If asked to think about an airship disaster, I expect most people would immediately call to mind the German Hindenburg and the loss of 36 lives in 1937, or the R101 crash of 1930 with 48 dead. In fact, the R38, at the time, the largest airship in the world has the dubious distinction of being the first of a series of deadly airship disasters. The airship had a complex ancestry.

Designed as R38 in England in 191, it was sold to the United States Navy before its completion early in 1921. As part of the handover, the British Government arranged to carry out 50 hours (the Americans wanted at least twice as much) of air trials over England and the North Sea. For their part, the US Navy would provide most of the air crew.

The writing was on the walls from the very first test in June 1921. In a seven-hour flight, serious balance issues were reported. Less than a month later, a second flight, closely followed by a third failed to complete resolve the problem and led to the failure of several structural support girders. These days, the idea that another, even more rigorous, test could be organised and carried out within a few days is unthinkable. But that is exactly what happened.

On 23rd August 1921 R38 departed from her base in Howden intending to moor at RNAS Pulham, Norfolk, which had a mast facility, unavailable at Howden. The idea was to conduct a two-day test including several challenging turns on the second day. Poor weather conditions made it impossible for R38 to be moored overnight as planned. Instead the airship was flown out over the North Sea, before returning for high-speed turning trials the following morning. By late afternoon, large crowds had gathered to watch the largest airship in the world as it flew back and forth over Hull turning sharply at speeds of up to 62 miles per hour. At just after half past five, the structure failed catastrophically. A reporter from the Hull Daily Mail picks up the story:

"A little before 5:40 … I stepped into Whitefriargate, when a violent explosion shocked and shook me. Never during the whole of the Zeppelin raids did I hear a crash so great, or a concussion so severe."

The reporter, clearly shaken, described how he hurried along Whitefriargate towards Victoria Square only to be stopped in his tracks once again:

"Barely had I taken half a dozen steps when there was another detonation and concussion every bit as heavy as the first. More windows crashed and fell."

By this time many were crying out that the airship had exploded. A police officer stood on Monument Bridge pointing towards a plume of smoke rising over the Humber. Like many others, the reporter rushed towards the pier where they all saw that what they feared really had happened:

"Round about floated masses of debris, still burning. Tugs and boats which had rushed out to the rescue, nosed about looking for survivors or for the bodies of those who were past human aid."

On the southern side of the Humber estuary at New Holland several more watched helplessly from the pier where travellers crossed between Hull and the Railway Station that connected them with all points south. Our reporter noted:

"it was the turn of the tide, dead low water, and the rearmost part of the airship had fallen across the shoal which intervenes between Hull and New Holland and rested there."

Later, it emerged that the five survivors all emerged from this section. Everyone else on board lost their lives. The reporter was able to interview (although he described it as a "chat") a man by the name of Martin, the Pier Master who noted that the airship *"came in with the wind, from the North East"*, and that her engines were *"working at a big speed"*. It was as if those on board knew that the airship was doomed and were rushing to avoid an even worse disaster over the heavily-populated city. In fact, eye witness accounts consistently described how the airship engines shrieked as the commander apparently built speed and aimed to take the buckling and bowing airship away from the city and over the water. It was only a matter of moments once R38 reached the estuary that the end came.

One witness recalled the scene:

"there was a terrible explosion, and the falling halves burst into flames. In a few seconds they reached the water, and then came a second explosion, as loud as the first."

Immediately, several boats moored at both Hull and New Holland Piers cast off and rushed to the rescue of any survivors. It was high summer and low water, but the Humber was ablaze and the airship had plummeted from an altitude of over 1,000 feet – about the same height as the twin towers of the original World Trade Center.

For the thousands now gathered on the Pier at Hull, the prospect of survivors being brought ashore must have appeared to be very remote. A tugboat, the *Englishman*, was the first to return to the pier, carrying a single crewman from R38:

"A red handkerchief, drenched with blood, covered his face and head ... to hide his shocking wounds."

People talked of him as being dead, but the reporter had spotted a *"slight heaving of the chest"* and knew otherwise. The newspaper correctly identified the victim as the *"commander of the ship"*, but A. H. Wann, was, in fact, a flight lieutenant, not a captain. The English skipper went on to recover from his wounds and advanced through the ranks of the Royal Air Force to Air Commodore.

Another survivor was Leading Aircraftman E. W. Davies who told reporters that as soon as the petrol tanks exploded *"it was all over in a moment ... some of the poor fellows had no chance"*.

Only five survived the disaster, four Britons and a sole American – all had been in the rear section of the airship. Bodies of the Americans that died were returned to the United States, but nine of the British bodies were buried in Hull. Should you visit the memorial, the names marked with a cross are those whose bodies lie beneath the monument.

The R38 disaster brought an immediate halt to the British Airship industry, and it also signals the end of this alphabetical guide to the Yorkshire Coast.

But not every end is final. Three years later and Airships were flying over Britain once again. Hopefully the parallel with this guide book does not include use of the word *disaster* for both. However, it does make me wonder if there is room in my life and perhaps yours for another journey through Yorkshire ... from A to Z.

Further Reading

Zeppelin Blitz: The German Air Raids on Great Britain during the First World War, Neil Storey, The History Press (2015)

Zeppelins of World War I, Wilbur Cross, Paragon House (1991)

Flight of the Titan, George Rosie, Birlinn Ltd. (2010)

A brief history of Hull in three sections (section 3 includes much of World War I
http://www.hullhistorycentre.org.uk/discover/hull_history_centre/about_us/historyofhull.aspx

Accompanied by numerous photographs, this site gives a good account of the Zeppelin raids on Hull and surrounding areas   http://www.paul-gibson.com/social-history/hull-in-the-first-world-war.php

Going Out?

When arriving at the seaside and taking that first magnificent look out to sea the same question always arises, regardless of whether or not it is spoken aloud. Is it coming in or going out? One of the myriads of marvels of creation is the tidal system. Up and down the Yorkshire coastline, whether you are at Saltburn, Scarborough or Spurn the tide will go out and come in twice every 24 hours and 50 minutes, in a pattern known as *semi-diurnal*. Not everywhere is like this. The Gulf of Mexico, for example has *diurnal* tides – only one high tide and one low tide in the same period. Since the Gulf of Mexico is not in Yorkshire just yet, we will only consider the semi-diurnal type.

Why 24 hours and 50 minutes, and not exactly 24 hours then? It's a matter of gravity. Water is affected by the gravitational forces applied by both our Sun and Moon. The Moon orbits us in the same direction as we spin and the time it takes for Earth to rotate exactly once relative to our Moon is 12 hours and 25 minutes. This is why we can sometimes observe the Moon, for example, in the same position in the sky in the early morning and in the evening on the same day. Broadly speaking, the nearer water is to the Moon, the more influence it's gravity has on it, and consequently, the higher the tide will be in that area. So, in Yorkshire, we get a high tide every 12 hours and 25 minutes. Furthermore, approximately twice every month, corresponding roughly to the times of new moon and full moon, the Sun, Moon and Earth fall into line with one another. A condition with the fantastic astronomical title of *syzygy*, derived from the ancient Greek word *σύζυγος* (pronounced *suzugos*) meaning "yoked together". An occurrence of syzygy can result in an eclipse, but will definitely lead to what is known as a *"spring tide"*. Many people mistakenly believe this to be associated with the season of the same name. Not so. The word *"spring"* in this instance relates to the other use of the word i.e. to jump, or rise or burst forth as in a natural spring.

So now we know why and when we can expect particularly high tides. What about the opposite? As you might expect, if we get very high tides when the Moon is full or new, we can anticipate that our lowest high tides will occur when the Moon is in its first and third quarter stages. This is because at these times, the Sun and the Moon are at right angles to the Earth and so their gravitational influences counteract one another to some extent and combine to have a weaker pull on the sea's waters. These go by the name of *neap tides*, with the word deriving from an Anglo-Saxon word meaning *"without power"*.

Finally, on this matter, and perhaps of interest to those who like to take a photograph or two of our Moon, we should remember that the Moon does not have a constant circular orbital path. Because it follows an elliptical orbit there are times when it will be nearer. The Moon at its closest is said to be at perigee. The opposite is apogee. When perigee combines with a new or full moon (usually three or four times every calendar year), we experience a *perigean spring tide* (known as a *king tide* in many parts of the world), causing the highest of high tides. The Moon itself, since it is closer than at other times, also appears up to 15% larger. In 2016, the full moons in the last three months of the year should be the best times for photographers to capture fantastic lunar photographs at high tide – weather permitting!

What is it about the tides that is so captivating? For me, it is the fact that the view changes, almost by the minute. A walk along the promenade in one direction at, say, Withernsea, or Bridlington can give a completely different view of the seafront than the return walk, perhaps a couple of hours later. I can recall pausing on the recently restored footbridge on Filey's lovely promenade with my wife, to admire the wide sandy beach and the view beyond Carr Naze to the Brigg and the Spittals exposed by the low tide. The only waves we could see were the white horses (Americans call them whitecaps) glistening in the sunshine way out to sea. Later on, we stood on the same footbridge and watched giant breakers crashing against the sea wall, showering us with spray and running up the cobbled road beneath us.

In fact, we shouldn't really talk in terms of *"the"* Yorkshire Coast, because use of the definite article tends to imply a singular thing, like *the* book, *the* car, *the* dog etc. Yet, wherever you end up on the Yorkshire Coast, you will find differences to the Yorkshire Coast just a minute or two away in either direction. Even, as we have just seen, the same location will be different from one moment to the next. And, that is the beauty of the coast, and the Yorkshire coast, in particular. No two places, in location, or time, are ever the same. There is something new to wonder at, wherever or whenever you happen to visit.

No two promenades are the same, piers all have their own unique characteristics, bays and harbours have their own personalities – just like the fishing folk have their own gansey patterns. Every community has a different history, and different stories to tell. Locations can even have their own distinctive micro-climate as the folk of Kilnsea and Spurn will tell you. Try standing atop Oliver's Mount on a summers day, for example. You might be able to see Whitby bathed in Sunshine, a sea mist over Flamborough Head and rainclouds over Malton inland all at the same time.

Over the years I have learned to appreciate the Yorkshire coast, not just for what it is, but for what it has been and what it is likely to become as well. To get a real sense of each locations past and its potential future as well as appreciating it for what is in front of my eyes. To understand what a place has experienced to be as it is these days and to be able to envision the same place in a few years' time. Even better to return to see the changes first hand, for example, by pacing to the cliff edge from the Blue Bell café at Kilnsea to measure how much has vanished since our last visit, or to walk along the front at Bridlington as the promenades continue to be redeveloped to meet the needs of twenty-first century tourism.

Returning finally to spring tides, when combined with stormy conditions they can have catastrophic consequences. Take this example from December 1917, reported in the *Hull Daily Mail*:

"The high wind caused the spring tide at Scarborough, on Monday, to rise to an unusual height and strength. It swept completely over the Foreshore roads, and the new Marine Drive. After it had receded the roads were covered with sand. Three lamp standards were broken, a workmen's hut destroyed and the doors of several North Side bather's bungalows were broken in."

On that occasion, no loss of life occurred. Eleven years earlier, the spring tide in March 1906 coincided with a great storm leading to serious consequences along much of the Yorkshire coast. You may wish to refer back to some of the maps to show you exactly how bad things got. At Staithes, homes and business premises were flooded as far as the old Post Office. At Robin Hood's Bay, the waves washed completely over the roof of the coastguard station, broke down the sea wall in front of the same building and flooding was widespread for a considerable distance up Station Road. The Robin Hood's Bay Hotel had several windows smashed in by the force of the waves. At Hornsea, the entire promenade gardens were washed away and flooding occurred inland as far as the Mere. There was also considerable damage to the groynes here and along the coast at Withernsea. Whitby possibly was the worst affected. Photographs taken at the time show giant waves smashing over both harbour walls and reaching the top of the lighthouse. The Whitby Gazette was able to provide its own eye-witness account of the flooding. Most low-lying streets were affected, and the waters even breeched their own premises in Grape Lane *"for the first time within recollection"*.

For some of those at sea, the stormy spring tide conditions had lethal consequences. The *SS Colne* had left Goole a day earlier, bound for Rotterdam laden with a cargo of coal and other goods. The steel steamship was only three years old, and at 235-feet in length was capable of carrying well over 500 tons safely. Little did they know at the time that they were heading straight into a night of storms *"when owing to the wildness of the weather the sea (would make) the greatest inroad on Holderness than is said to have been the case for hundreds of years"*. Twelve of the 17 crew were lost the following day when the ship sank in conditions described to the subsequent inquiry by surviving crew members as *"the roughest any of them remembered in the North Sea"*.

As we take in the majesty of our great Yorkshire coastline we should continually respect the power that lies so frequently apparently dormant almost within our reach, but never within our grasp. The sea is a wonderful sight. Ever changing, ever inspiring, ever dangerous. There are thousands of places and hundreds of different ways to enjoy the Yorkshire coast – but you don't need to risk life and limb to do so. Please take care. That way you can get pleasure from this beautiful area over and over again.

So there you have it. My take on the Yorkshire Coast from A to Z. There will be hundreds, if not thousands of wonderful locations that didn't get a mention. Whether you renewed an interest in an old favourite or two, or maybe visited a few new places, I hope the guide has been and will continue to be useful. I will try to keep the map pages as up to date as possible, so please do as I do with the Yorkshire Coast and come back regularly.

Printed in Poland
by Amazon Fulfillment
Poland Sp. z o.o., Wrocław